IN OUR OWN
WORDS
IN OUR OWN
PICTURES

compiled by Valley and Vale
financed by Associated British Ports

July 1989

We gratefully acknowledge previous publication
of the poems used in this book and the copyright
thereof:

Barry Island by John Idris Jones appeared in *Barry
Island & Other Poems* published by John Jones Ltd.

Let's go to Barry Island, Maggie Fach by Idris
Davies is from his *Collected Poems,* published by
Gwasg Gomer.

Gillian Clarke's poems are taken from *Letting in
Rumour,* her new collection, published this year
by the Carcanet.

Lines at Barry by Tony Curtis are taken from his
Selected Poems 1970-1985 (Poetry Wales Press).
Home Front is taken from *The Last Candles,*
published by Seren Books.

ISBN 0 9514831 0 2

Ordinary people are the only real experts in the histories of their lives; not always perhaps in the dates and timings of exactly what happened where - facts which progressively fade over time - but much more importantly in the feelings, the attitudes and the values which illustrate and underpin the changes that have occured. It is the apparently insignificant memories - the personal triumphs, the tragedies, the moments of humour and of pain - narrated here, that tell more about what it meant to live and work in Barry over the last one hundred years than volumes of dry historical fact. Iorwerth Prothero's recollections of the outbreak of World War One and the food queues that followed; David Wiltshire's wonderful Armistice Day story; Phyllis John's short but finely drawn picture of family life and discipline; Jack Stevens' memories of Leon Vint and his Electric Palace in Thompson Street; Elizabeth Sharman's recollections of the soup kitchens of the 1926 strike; Elsie Phipps' and Phyllis Caldwell's early introduction to the harsh world of "service" and the roles and rights of women; George Storey's "promotion" to medical representative following just two lessons with the St. John's Ambulance service; Maureen Flipse's recollections of the "miners' fortnights" on Barry Island and of the heyday of Thompson Street; and all the other memories "IN OUR OWN WORDS - IN OUR OWN PICTURES" reveal more about the realities of life in Barry than all the dates and documents which normally become the official record of a town's existence.

That is why this book uses the eyes and ears of the people of Barry to describe the often turbulent history of the town. (The text is condensed from over fifty hours of interviews with local people and with a few who have left Barry but still retain their memories of the town). That is why the photographs - each one an irreplaceable chapter in the history of South Wales - are for the most part from people's own private collections, some published here for the first time.

As well as those mentioned above, we would like to thank all the many people who have given generously of their time and/or work throughout the various stages in the shaping of this book. I hope, in this long list, that we don't leave anyone out:

Austin Michael Bower, Ken Caldwell, Christine Clarke, Gillian Clarke, Tom Clemett, Viv Corbin, Tony Curtis (for suggesting the poems), the late Idris Davies, Jim Davies, Leonard Davies, the late Sam Demery, Hector Downes, Chris Foster (of Mobile Arts), Ashley Griffiths, Frank Hodges, F.C. Hortop, Gareth Howe, Chris Humphreys, Donna Jones (for help with some of the printing), John Idris Jones, Glyn Kitcatt for the fine pen and ink drawings (Glyn would like to thank Mr. G. Deighton for giving him access to various archive materials without which many of the illustrations could not have been executed), Brian Luxton, Bob Martin, William Mitchell, John O'Beirne, Ralph Phillips (editor, Barry and District News), Aubrey Pittard-Davies, Marjorie Prothero, Harry Press, Paul Rabane, D.W. Roberts, W.F. Roberts, W.E. Rogers, the late H. Shirvington, Dr. Storr, the South Glamorgan Library Service, Mary Thomas, D.H. Williams, J.O. Williams, Iorwerth Williams, Stuart Wilson (ABP), Dai Woodham and The Woodlands Centre, Barry.

And finally, extra special thanks to Jack Stevens and to George Storey, without whom this book would not have become a reality.

Valley and Vale, July 1989

based at
Holm View Centre,
Gibbonsdown,
BARRY CF6 3DA
Tel Barry 742289

"In recognition of the long relationship between the Docks and the town of Barry, Associated British Ports is pleased to be associated with Valley and Vale in the publication of this illustrated collections of personal anecdotes and reminiscences."

Port Manager, Cardiff/Barry

1

"It is an odd thing that in a rock by the sea where one first lands on the island, there is a small crack. If you press your ear to it, you can hear a noise like that of blacksmiths at work, the blowing of bellows, the strokes of hammers and the harsh grinding of files on metal."

Gerald of Wales 1188

Working on the Junction Cut, a waterway between Dock No. 1 and 2

William Spickett mending a barrel, Cadoxton stream

In 1882, Parliament sanctioned proposals of Lord Bute to increase the shipping charges at Cardiff. These extra shipping charges were made up of a ha'penny per ton for shunting and a ha'penny per ton for the use of the storage sidings. Although these two ha'pennies were never charged, the threatened imposition of this increase was sufficient to cause a body of freighters to decide to undertake construction of whatever further Dock accommodation was necessary at their own expense . . .

Glenavon Colliery, Blaengarw

".....there had been such a tremendous increase in the amount of coal exported from Cardiff and Penarth docks that the Taff Vale Railway was absolutely jammed with traffic, to such an extent that it was a common sight to find coal trains stretched nose to tail all the way from Penarth docks right up to the old Walnut Street viaduct. Engine drivers on the Taff Vale railway should have taken something like two and a half hours to travel from the Rhondda down to the docks when the docks were quiet, but when the docks were busy it was not uncommon for them to be on their trains from anything up to twelve to fifteen hours making the short or comparatively short journey to Cardiff. If the railway was like that then, of course, the docks must have been as bad. People nowadays do not realise that it was quite a common sight to find anything from two hundred to three hundred ships lying at anchor in the Penarth Road, waiting to get into the Cardiff Docks .....

......The situation became so desperate that the coal freighters led by that great Welsh entrepreneur, David Davies of Llandinam, and assisted by the Earl of Plymouth, by the Jenner family of Wenvoe, by Lord Romilly and others, decided that the time had come to build a dock elsewhere."

Leonard Davies

"When the Barry Docks and Railways Bill appeared before the House of Commons Committee in 1883, the opponents of the Bill, the Taff Vale Railway Company, had a Mr. Bidder Q.C., and a Mr. Pope. Mr. Pope gave evidence seated. He had a sylvan voice and was a very searching questioner. On one occasion, David Davies was asked where he could get money to build a dock at Barry. The questioner doubted that a man who had been a sawyer at the beginning of his career could find sufficient money to build a dock. David Davies, in a righteous wrath, replied that he was not a sawyer, but a Top-Sawyer, the man who stood at the top of the saw-pit, and that he would be very pleased to send the money up in coal trucks, in gold sovereigns to Parliament if they wanted to have sight of it. The dock was eventually built and on the 18th July 1889, was opened when the S.S. Arno sailed in through the dock gates, followed by the S.S. Ravenshoe."

Leonard Davies

"As our representative at yesterday's proceedings so aptly put it, the cutting of the first sod of the Barry Dock and Railway was an auspicious ceremony. Symbolically, it signalled the end of an heroic struggle, not least in Parliament, on the part of the promoters of the Scheme, under the dauntless and inspiring leadership of Mr David Davies M.P. It was also a symbol of great things to come in these ancient parishes of Barry, Cadoxton and Merthyr Dyfan. Soon, their green fields will begin to disappear as the new and important seaport of Barry grows apace. A time of unimaginable change lies ahead. As well as homes for the tens of thousands of people who are confidently expected to settle in Barry, vital facilities will have to be provided. Hospitals, schools, shops and offices, all will have to be built. In addition, roads, sewers, and supplies of gas and water will have to be provided. The mind reels at the magnitude of the challenge that confronts us. We have no doubt, however, that the challenge will be met. For our own part we are determined, once the population of the town warrants it, to strive for the establishment of a Public Library in Barry, preferably in the most central location possible. For, in the time-honoured tradition of local newspapers, we believe passionately in the need for an informed public. To further this same end we are determined too, to set up our own offices in the most central position possible when the new town has taken shape. On present estimates, that means that we should be established in the heart of Barry no later than the year 1889. At the heart, we shall be well placed to act as a true sounding board for the people of Barry.

Experience shows that the offices of a local newspaper are perhaps the most frequented place in any town. Scores, maybe hundreds, of people will surely visit us at our new offices each week, to pour forth their feelings on this or that issue of the day; and it will be on the basis of their feelings that we shall promulgate our views. We shall never succumb to the pressures of any particular group, whose sound and fury may well be out of all proportion to the worthiness of their cause. Such groups have always existed and, doubtless, their like will still be in existence one hundred years hence.

What Barry will be like one hundred years hence is impossible to visualize. It is impossible, for example, to say with any certainty whether coal, that invaluable mineral on which Barry will be built, will still be in such abundant demand in 1984. If it is not, what trade will there be to support and sustain Barry Dock? If it were not too fanciful, one could half-seriously conjecture that it might be in some new-fangled commodity like chemicals, or in exotic fruit from some distant lands! More seriously, the one thing that can be said with certainty is that Barry in 1984 will not be the Barry that we shall shortly see. Great and terrible wars may have intervened to change the whole order of things as we now know it. New minerals, new sources of combustion may have been discovered, to render less vital the vast reserves of coal we are told lie beneath the South Wales Valleys. And, inevitably there will have been great changes in the political and industrial life of this nation, and sweeping changes in the patterns of its social life. One hundred years hence, therefore, Barry may well be compelled to undertake a major reappraisal of its role. If that shall be the case, we have this advice for the people of Barry in 1984: Do not be afraid to change, so long as it is not change for its own sake, and so long as what is good and fine in our inheritance is not carelessly cast aside. Change there must, perforce, be. If we to undertake a major reappraisal today, in 1884, were to set against the bold and imaginative transformations that have been proposed for this community, there would be no great town of Barry in 1984."

"November 15th, 1884 Editorial" which appeared in Barry and District News November 15th, 1984

"Mr. John Wolf Barry was the engineer for the construction of the dock, later to become Sir John Wolf Barry, assisted by H.M. Brunel, a son of Isambard Kingdom Brunel, the eminent Victorian engineer. The contractor for the building of the dock was Thomas Andrew Walker who had recently completed the construction of the Severn Tunnel, and was currently engaged in the construction of Preston Docks, the Manchester Ship Canal and the Buenos Aires docks. He was one of the great contractors of the last century......"

Leonard Davies

Construction of No. 1 Docks

'We have five million tons of coal, and we can fill a thundering good dock the first day we open it."

David Davies,
House of Commons,
1882

"In 1884, my grandfather, Captain Richard Davies, applied for the post of Dockmaster at the new docks building at Barry, and was successful in his application.....He took up his post......in August, 1888. His remit, at that time, was to oversee the installation of dock equipment, to recruit staff and train them, and to take in hand the details of dock working. He took up lodgings in newly built High Street, leaving his family in Penarth, while the new family house in Romilly Road was being built. And on completion of this, the rest of the family moved to Barry. On July 18th, 1889, the ceremonial opening of Barry Docks took place. The organisation of this event was in the hands of the Dockmaster and his staff, and a photograph taken of the dignitaries present before the official cutting of the ribbon, shows my grandfather in the middle of the group. The ribbon, a red, white and blue silk ribbon was cut with a dagger of Damascus steel by Mrs. Lewis Davies of Ferndale. And after the ceremony, this was cut into segments and presented to the dignitaries present. We still have our particular segment in good order, I am pleased to say."

Aubrey Pittard-Davies

"...My father was born in the village of Clanfield in Oxfordshire. And things were very bad......not much work....and they realised that there was going to be a new docks built at Barry and so three of them thought they would go down there and look for work - my father, his cousin, and a third person.

And they walked all the way from Clanfield which is near Fairford aerodrome down to Barry. Now when my father got here, the first job that he got was as a coachman to the Reverend Ebenezer Morris, who was the rector of the Cadoxton parish, St. Cadoc's church.....

My father was quite satisfied and so was his cousin but the third person, he didn't like Barry so he decided he'd go back, and he walked all the way back to Oxfordshire; he'd had enough of Barry. But the other two, my father and his cousin, both became plate-layers and one became the Chief Permanent Way Inspector of the Barry Railway Company, and he was there until he died.

...my mother was born in the village of Fivehead near Ilminster in Somerset. And the same thing applied there, very little work....and they heard there was work in this area.....Cardiff Docks, and there was something at Penarth, so they came over.....

...my mother said she'd never been outside the village. She'd never been near the sea, she had no idea what it was like. And he took them to Weston-super-Mare, to catch the boat to come across to Cardiff, and when they got to Weston-super-Mare, they walked out on the pier and my mother said - she's told me this so often , 'We were scared stiff, I'd never seen the sea, and when we were walking on the pier, I looked down and I could see the water through the cracks between the planks on the pier, and we were hanging onto my parents for grim death, till we got to the boat. The boat took us to Cardiff'."

Jack Stevens

"I'm from Porthleven in Cornwall, and I was brought here as a little girl. My mother came with nine boys and three girls and she had another little girl in her fiftieth year. We were a wonderful family - never, ever quarelled."
Elizabeth Sharman.

"My father, when he was living at St. Dogmaels, Cardigan, started on an apprenticeship as a shoeing smith, but when my father got a job in Barry, the family moved up and he finished his apprenticeship under the old Barry Railway Company, still as a blacksmith. Blacksmiths were not always shoeing smiths. It's very easy to make a transition from a shoeing smith to a blacksmith working in docks, railway offices or in a chain works, very easy, because a lot of it was forging work, so he finished his apprenticeship by about 1903 or 4."
Iorwerth Prothero

SOUTH WALES PHOTOGRAPHIC CO.,
266, HOLTON ROAD, BARRY DOCK.

8

Wedding of Eluned Davies, Jim's aunt, to William Griffiths, Jerusalem Chapel, Barry, 1929

"My grandfather, aged fifteen and an orphan from Llanon in Cardiganshire, walked to Barry in 1876 to seek his fortune. By 1890, he had secured his own tailor's shop, London House in Holton Road, and the business employed six tailors specialising in gents' suits. My grandmother, Catherine Jones, came to Barry from Pontrhydfendigaid, Cardiganshire, I believe, as a servant. This is a picture of both of them with their first son, my father, Dan.''

Jim Davies

Dan Davies, Jim's father, with cousin Norman Richards on holiday in Weston-super-Mare, about 1920

9

"At the opening of the dock, there was a big banquet. When the guests came to sit down, Thomas Andrew Walker could not be found and a search was made....At the other end of the dock there was a marquee with all the navvies who had built the dock sitting under the chairmanship of Walker enjoying a lunch, and this is the measure of the man, a remarkable contractor far in advance of his age, a man who cared for the navvies who worked for him. At Barry he built Queen Street, Princes Street and the north side of High Street as accommodation for the navvies and their families who were working on the docks. At the back of the present Barclays Bank was East Barry House taken over by Walker as a hospital and used as such for any accidents that happened during the building of the dock.

And accidents did happen. When they were working on the Barry Island side of the dock, the old harbour part of it, the horses suddenly panicked one day at lunch time and took off. The cliff face collapsed trapping a number of navvies underneath. He also provided a school at numbers 56-7 Queen Street for the children of the navvies....The Mission Hall in Barry is now a Cash and Carry store but was at one time the Welsh Congregational Chapel in High Street. My father always referred to that chapel as Walker's Hall. Services were held two or three times a week.

...He was far in advance of his time as an employer who really cared for his employees."
Leonard Davies

"Dad used to go to sea and he saw Barry Docks being built, when there was no Phyllis Street, nothing like that. One day he came up the Ship Hill to go into the Marine Hotel for a pint... he used to like to have a glass of beer with the other men ... and he saw these houses being built in Phyllis Street, the top end, and he put his name down. And I don't know whether he said it was a shilling or a half a crown he put down. But just imagine a beautiful home, and they were well built. They're still there, I suppose, I haven't seen them for years. And everytime he came in port, he used to put more money down until he had enough to buy the house."
Elizabeth Sharman

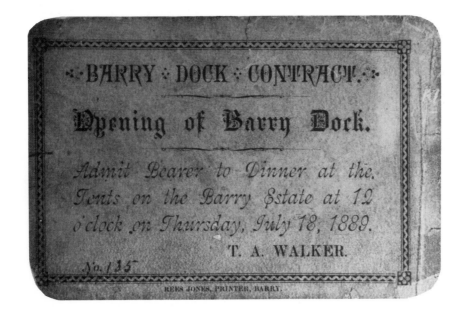

"The Ferguson, I was told ..... she struck the wall when she was coming in. And it was a good many years later that I actually came across this photograph which proves how off-course she was......you can see there's a wire from the stern to a tug-boat which was holding her. Ships coming into the Dock entrance from the Channel have to allow for the very strong currents outside of Barry which send a ship sideways.....Now what I think happened was, he's got into the Basin here and he was going into the Dock and he must have been pushed over on one side and the tug here, you can see, holding her, lost control a bit and she's gone smack into the wall instead of going in through there and you can see that the captain and the pilot on board realised she was going, put her full steam astern......"
Jack Stevens

"The dock, as you know, is still fast filling with ships. We have the finest dock in the world and when we have improved the entrance a little more within the next three or four months...(it) ...will be impossible for a ship to go wrong....You have heard, no doubt, a little talk as to the difficulty of getting in on the part of a few not accustomed to the place. In fact, these foreigners are half mad. When they see the great dock they think it is the Mediterranean and they go at full speed at the gate. The ship comes into collision with some part of the dock and, of course, the ship gets the worst of it."
David Davies, 1899

"Barry town was brought into being by the Docks. You had to have houses for workers, you had to have shops for the workers, you had to have entertainment for the workers, the churches, the chapels; you had to have the roads; you had to have local government; you had to have estate agents, doctors, all the services......"
Iorwerth Prothero

The original caption to this picture read "Barry Dock, Cardiff"!

"The docks expanded and prospered very rapidly, and in 1898, two events took place: the first the completion and opening of No. 2 dock, and second the opening of the deep water lock or Lady Windsor Lock. Both of these events were opened without ceremony but were followed by a large dinner at the Barry Hotel. The lock took five years to build, having been started in 1893, and all the excavation, blasting and dredging of the space required by the lock was carried out by the Dock-master's staff, under the command of my grandfather and Mr. James Bell, the engineer. The masonry work was done by Sir John Jackson's firm. In all, 84,000 cubic yards of material were removed to a depth of 18 feet. below spring tide low water line. At the completion of the project, an official photograph was taken in the empty lock, with my grandfather in the centre of the group of dignitaries and with the massive lock gates in the picture behind."

Aubrey Pittard-Davies

"I can remember as a boy, every coal hoist was occupied. The tier was packed with steamers awaiting their turn to be loaded, with more shipping laying out in the 'roads' (i.e. the Bristol Channel), unable to be accommodated in the Docks themselves. Coal was being loaded right around the clock - with no let up. I remember too a very lucrative trade with the import of pit props from Russia - 'the Black Sea trade' as it was called. A ship would leave with coal and return with props, eagerly awaited by the 'prop workers'. Other steamers would be arriving with wheat for the flour mills, frozen meat for the cold stores; a journey out with coal and a quick trip back with other merchandise."
Frank Hodge

a "large, rapidly-growing town, intent on nothing but money-making...."
Llewellyn Williams, Liberal M.P., on Barry, 1892

"...the Porthkerry viaduct was started in 1894 and in 1896, two of the piers, 10 and 11, subsided about a couple of feet and this added about six months to the completion period. And what they found was that the foundations of these piers and No. 12 had not been taken down to the solid rock. They also found that pier 13, the other side of the path now, hadn't been taken down to the solid rock, but they did nothing at all about that. So, the viaduct and the railway was opened on December 1st, 1897, and then there was a lot of heavy rain and on the 10th of January, 1898, the pier 13 ....subsided about 2ft. and the viaduct was rather twisted. Well, when they came to examine the viaduct they found a lot of shoddy work in the foundations in particular, and behind the arches of the viaduct, and the viaduct had almost to be completely remade. They put the new concrete in, in stages -'toothing' it was called - part of the foundations would have the new concrete and they cut out the old bit. The result is that the viaduct was closed for nearly two years to passenger traffic and one and a quarter years for goods traffic.

There is a slight cant to the viaduct to the North; it's so slight but it's stood up to traffic for the last 89 years, so there's no harm done."

Iorwerth Prothero

"My grandfather came to Barry to work on the building of the railway viaduct, which runs over Porthkerry Park - and when he finished that, he applied for a dock porter's licence. He had enough money to buy a horse and cart, and he applied for a dock porter's licence to carry the bags of the seamen to and from the ships. And eventually, he had an accident - I can't quite tell you when he had it - but then my father, who was his eldest son, was granted his licence as a docks porter. And he was a docks porter right up until 1936, when, as the number of ships fell away, he applied for a marine stores dealer's licence, which in those days was known as a 'junkie's' licence, because we bought junk. He bought bamboos, he bought whale oil - he used to have to strip off if he bought whale oil, in the bilges, because, you know what whale oil's like, apart from anything else, the smell and God knows what. And he'd strip off and bale the whale oil into 40 gallon barrels. We never sold the whale oil. We used to boil that up and put caustic salt with it to make our own soap."

Dai Woodham

Porthkerry Viaduct

"My uncle was a wagon examiner on Barry Station, he tapped the wheels of the engine. He used to see men coming from the Head Office, and got to know them. One day he mentioned to them he'd like his 'son' to come and work for the Docks and they said, 'Well, send him over for the examination and we'll see if he's suitable.' My birthday was the 5th of July, a Friday, I had my fourteenth birthday - you left school at fourteen then - and he told me I had to go over the office on Saturday and have a look at this examination. I passed the examination. They told me at 11 o'clock I start work on Monday...so Friday I had my birthday; Saturday, I sat the exam; Sunday I went to church; Monday I went to work. I actually started work on July 8th, 1918."

David Wiltshire

"My parents came here because there was work here, the Docks were here. Coming up to the war, it was good money. They could work all the hours they liked to."

Phyllis John

No. 1 Dock. – 1911

"And the Bennetts, and the Burfords, of course, their dads were pilots ......they ran the pilot boats you know ....and kids quarrel, you know, and they said, 'My dad's a pilot'. I said, 'That's nothing.' I said, 'My father is a pilot's assistant'. I thought that was one up and it was one down."

Elizabeth Sharman

"I used to take my father's meals down to him. And as they saw me coming along the path to the No. 7 tip, they used to say, 'Here she is, on time as usual'. I had to be on time, didn't I, because I had to go back to school.

And he'd come down and give me a handful of tiny, tiny nuts that had come in as ballast in the ships, they used to bring them home, these monkey nuts ...sweet as anything, you could eat all the outside as well. And he'd give me a handful, you know, and you'd eat them on the way home."

Phyllis Caldwell

Shipping Superintendents Staff, 1898

"I went to work on the Dock until I was 16, provisionally just filling in time. I went to work for a wagon repairing firm, that repaired all the coal wagons that came to Barry Docks. And I started there as a screw boy.

Now a screw boy was the lowest of the low in that industry because what it meant was that when the wagons were being repaired the bolts were taken out and because of the war you couldn't get new bolts and things to go back into the wagons, so you had a lathe, a screwing lathe, and put a new thread on the bolts. It was a dirty, wet, unpleasant job which broke every factory act ever written. But I did it for nine months, then I graduated to office boy at No.4 tip on No.1 dock. The men who worked in this industry - you talk about it being hard on the dock - these were some of the hardest men I ever met; they had to be because the work was tremendously difficult.....

There wasn't a man who was there who hadn't suffered one serious physical injury in his life from the job he was doing. One or two were really maimed and had to retire......And they were on piece-work during the war which meant that they had to work very hard to earn a reasonable wage."

George Storey

"To the left, you can see a coffee tavern with the name Solomon Andrews on it. He was a confectioner from Newbury in ·Wiltshire, born in 1835 and came to Cardiff about 1840 or thereabouts. He was a remarkable man. He had an enormous range of business activities -confectionary, cakes, anything connected with hauling, coaches, cabs, buses, taxis, he opened shops, undertaker's business, he designed coaches - he is supposed to have been the originator of the staircase you found on London buses in the 1920's, supposed to have been developed at his workshop in Cardiff.

He always used to sit down when the hymn which begins, 'With pity I look down on the riches here below'. He always sat down when that was sung because he never looked with pity on his riches and when a fellow councillor, Snook, used to stand up, he always said to Snook, 'Sit down, you don't believe that, do you?' ''

Iorwerth Prothero

"History is pictures. Unfortunately, no matter how you care for your prized possessions, time fades. How wonderful, therefore, to be able to print photographs taken seventy to eighty years ago, from the original negatives, and bring them up as fresh and new as if they had been taken only yesterday!

For this we are indebted to one Sam Demery, a well known resident of Barry Island, who himself was a keen amateur photographer. Over the years, he collected some hundred and fifty of these negatives, covering Barry and surrounding areas. Some he took himself, but a great many were obviously obtained through Bert Shirvington, the man whose cameras were responsible for much of the pictorial history of Barry. The negatives were given to me by Mrs. May Demery (Sam's widow), who decided at ninety-one years of age that she needed a change of scenery and left for the high life in Torquay. She is still hale and hearty and lives with daughter, Val, and son-in-law, Graham.

The negatives are of plate glass, seven inches by five inches, and most of them were used for making postcards, (five inches by three-and-a-half-inches), for commercial purposes. To get them to this size, this meant you actually lost fifty percent of the pictures originally taken. We, therefore, decided that we would remove the masking and present the photographs in their full size. In some cases this was very difficult, hence the marks showing the edge of the photographs and the black strip that originally showed the heading. However, we are sure that the extra detail revealed is well worth it."

George Storey

Baileys Commercial Dry Dock, First World War

Children's Party in the Colonial Club, Thompson Street

"Thompson Street in those days was reputed to be the richest road in the country, where every nationality worked and lived cheek by jowl - Greeks, Italians, Spaniards, Jews, Arabs, Norwegians. Coffee shops, outfitters, ships' chandlers, a shooting range, and fish and chip shops - a cutlet of hake and chips for three old pennies - barbers, tobacconists, banks, you name it, it was all in dear old Thompson Street. There was a cinema (now a car park), where the first 'talkie' was shown: 'Who killed Jack Donovan ?' I can remember seeing it, and to me it was little short of something of a marvel. Then there were the seamen's boarding houses of all nationalities, and the 'donkey's breakfast' manufacturers (i.e. makers of sailors' beds - ticking covers or bags stuffed with straw costing half a crown, or three and sixpence with extra straw), an Arab mosque, butchers' and chemist's shops, and yes, brothels too."

Frank Hodge

Committee of the Colonial Club, inc. Mr. Abbey Farrah, "the father of Cardiff and Barry Docks"

Mrs. Flipse's children and friends, Thompson Street, 1956

Mrs. Violet Jones' son, Phillip, 1950's

"There were various nationalities there and they all had
their own boarding houses and cafes and meeting places,
you know, as the British would do if they were abroad;
everyone wants to be with their own and yet everyone
mixed.
When I was young, one didn't hear words like ethnic or
racial - you just lived in the area and were part of the
area."

Maureen Flipse.

"When it was decided to develop Barry Dock, they knocked it down. There was a lot of thoughts about that. What a shame that that history of Barry is gone..... When I realised...... I thought that the best thing to do is get a record of the demolition of the street....and so I went up at intervals and took several pictures of the old buildings in process of demolition....."

Jack Stevens

August, 1972

Twentieth Century Club delegation to League of Nations, Geneva, 1932

2

"That's the way they were made."

".....my sister stayed home to help my mother with the children. My other sister went doing housework with somebody in Windsor Road. And I was sent down to take a message to her. And I was horrified ....she had a big tin bath. Oh, it was huge and a load of washing and a lot of dirty woollies. I said, 'You don't do all this?'
'Yes, I do.'
I said to her, 'How much do you get?'
'Six shillings a week'. 'Six bob', she said, 'six bob a week. And I give our mam five and I have one.'
I said, 'You've got to do all this for that?' And I can remember, the Christmas trimmings in this house in Windsor Road. 'I'm not doing it, I'm not doing housework like that.' And I didn't. I went nursing. I wasn't going to do that at any price."

Phyllis Caldwell

"I started work on the May 1st, 1921. And it was hard to get a job. I wanted to go and work in a draper's shop. I went everywhere. No, there were no jobs and not even to be an apprentice. Well, my mother didn't have ten pounds. So the one day we were in Madge Evans' and my mother asked her if she had a vacancy for an apprentice and she said, 'Well, I do want one really, but the thing is the money.' My mother misunderstood her. She thought she meant she couldn't afford to pay much and our Mam said - she always looked ahead, you know - 'Well, it's not the money so much as getting her in somewhere to be learning something.' 'Ooh,' she said, 'do you mean that?' And our Mam said, 'Yes', thinking I was going to have less than what was usual. Instead of that I was to work six months for nothing, and that's how I started work. Six months for nothing! And I was there five months and I was called up to the office. Oh, I thought she was going to finish me and start somebody else - another six months for nothing - but instead of that it was to commend me for my work, and particularly my personality. She said, 'The customers think that you're the tops - you're always nice to them -you always meet them as they come in the door and put a chair for them to sit down.' So she said, 'We've decided to keep you on and you'll get three shillings a week'. It was only years afterwards that the penny dropped - 'Don't come up for any this week', she said, 'you'll have to keep a week in hand'. I'd worked five months for nothing and I had to put a week in hand to get three shillings."

Elsie Phipps

"I was a domestic all my life, from the time I left school. In fact, I used to go in between school hours to one place. Cleaning and cooking and what not, for an elderly couple. You had to work harder than now. They don't know they're born today, with all the modern things they've got. But good luck to them. I don't blame them making it as easy as they can."

Phyllis John

"The Twentieth Century Club was started in 1902 by Dr. E.P. Hughes who had come to retire in Barry. And she used to gather together a group of her friends, men and women. And from that, the Club grew larger and larger until they had well over 130 members. At that time, I think, they were all women.... It was quite unique - there couldn't have been anything for women to belong to except meetings with their churches. Because women weren't involved in politics - they had no vote, they had to wait another twenty years before they had a vote."

Marjorie Prothero

"Mrs. Edgar Jones, a very active member, a past president of the Twentieth Century Club, who enthusiastically supported the League of Nations, took a party out in the very early days -the inauguration, perhaps ? She took a large party of women (from Barry) out to Geneva. It was very early days to be going and touring Europe, especially in a very large party ....That was in 1932. Women like Dr. E.P. Hughes were not confined to the four walls of their home, they did other things outside. Mrs. Digby Smith organised a pageant in the Memorial Hall on some famous women in history - she was another person who didn't just stay at home doing housework, sitting by the fireside."

Marjorie Prothero

"Now in the 1920's and even before.....it would be a very common sight to have the whole of the Docks covered in a great cloud of black coal dust ....if the wind ever got around to the east, which it frequently did during the winter months. I well remember my mother used to dash to the back of our home, which was in St. Nicholas Road, Barry, and close all the windows in order to stop the coal dust from blowing into the house."

Leonard Davies.

"In 1922, I'd just gone up to the county school.....I'd passed the scholarship. With that, a boat had come in from Russia into No. 2 Dock. They all thought it was jaundice....The chappie I was living with, Glover, he was the skipper and his first mate was living next door, his boy. His name was Knox, Barry Knox. Anyway, they brought a tropical disease doctor, that was Reynolds. He came down. He said, 'They got smallpox.' Right, so they whipped him off and me and the crew down to the Smallpox Hospital ...it's the College of Further Education now. Anyway, I went down there.
He died. I had smallpox. So I got pox marks here and there. Look at my face. I lived, other chaps lived, that poor little devil died.
That was 1922. Everybody in Barry then was wearing red ribbons, all around their arms ....innoculated, you see....And I had to go down and see the doctor and the surgery was full. Well, I had a red ribbon and my sister said, 'I've brought my brother here. He's just come out of the smallpox hospital. He's had smallpox.' Within two seconds flat, the surgery was empty, empty! And old Dr. Neale came out and he said, 'Are you feeling better? ....Where's all the surgery?'
'Well, we just told them I had smallpox'.
'Oh', he said, 'You'd better come again."

Ken Caldwell

"Around 1944/45 it was specified by the Factory Act that every work should have a medical representative for every twenty employees. The fact that I had just joined St. John's Ambulance and had had two lessons qualified me as a medical representative for this particular company on the Dock. Although I was only 15 years of age, no matter what the injury or whatever happened in the works, it was me who was called to attend. I saw broken legs, smashed ribs, anything you can think of...I was sitting in my office one day at lunch time and we had the old fashioned sloping desks and I was sitting there eating my sandwiches and I heard the door open behind me. I didn't turn round because, of course, people were in and out all the time and suddenly something flashed past my ear and landed on the paper that I was reading, just by my sandwiches. And a voice behind me said 'There you are, son. Put that in your sandwich'. And it was half a finger. I had to bandage it and get the ambulance to take him to hospital, but they were tough ....these men."

George Storey

"Timber was very scarce during the war, of course. For repairing the wagons, they used mainly oak cut straight from the forest and it was terrible to handle. And then towards the end of the war, they were importing keruing which is a Malayan oak, which wouldn't be allowed anywhere near anybody these days because if you got a splinter from keruing, if you didn't get the splinter out within an hour, an hour and a half, it would practically poison your whole system. So I spent many hours taking out splinters from anything from a quarter of an inch to one and a half inches long out of people's ....every part of their anatomy. I got to be an expert....quite often they used to sit on the timber as well...so I used to operate on a few rear ends."

"Half past four one afternoon, finishing time, one man came in and his nose was smashed all over his face. So I said to him 'What happened ?' 'Oh,' he said, 'a steel door on the bottom of the wagon fell on me'. And I said, 'We'll have to get you up to the hospital.' 'Oh, I'll go and change first,' he said. 'I got the bike, I can't leave the bike. I need it in the morning. I'll go home first.' So he turned round to go out the door and I said, 'Hang on. You got a bit of blood on the back.' And he was wearing this old peak cap. So I lifted his cap off and about two pints of blood ran out. He had this six inch gash at the back of the neck which ended up with 38 stitches. And he still wouldn't let me do anything. He wanted to go home first before going to hospital. That's the way they were made."

George Storey

The first school in Barry met at Nos. 57 and 58 Queen Street. On the right is a picture of the class of 1888.

"I was taught by maiden ladies - there was no married women. In fact, if you were teaching in Glamorgan, and you got married, marriage broke your contract, you weren't allowed to continue teaching. Only maiden ladies were allowed - and, of course, there were a lot of them, 'cos a lot of them lost their fiancees in the first world war. Then, during the [second world] war, married women were employed. We found this strange."

Mary Thomas

Porthkerry School

"My headmaster - on Barry Island - he ought to have been killed. Well I have, I've killed him many times, 'cos if you didn't stand in the hall with your two toes definitely together, not one toe out like that, he'd cut you with the cane. Oh, you know, his children were afraid of him and he had lovely children....."
Elizabeth Sharman

what could your Redeemer do, More than he hath done for you.

Elizabeth Jones Porthkerry School Aged 11 years 1850

Harvest Festival, Cadoxton School, 1907

Barbell and flag drill, Cadoxton school, October, 1899

"In school, the language of instruction was English and if the children spoke Welsh - like my father's family, they were brought up in Welsh - they were caned, boys and girls as well. But, of course, they were caned so frequently it didn't hurt much after a bit."
Iorwerth Prothero

Barry Intermediate School, 1913

"I am a great admirer of the old Welsh language, and I have no sympathy with those who would revile it. Still, I have seen enough of the world to know that the best medium to make money by is the English Language. I want to advise every one of my countrymen to master it perfectly; if you are content with brown bread, you can, of course, remain where you are. If you wish to enjoy the luxuries of life, with white bread to boot, the only way to do so is by learning English as well. I know what it is to eat both."
David Davies, National Eisteddfod, 1865

Porthkerry School

One of the very few early double decker buses in Barry. This Leyland was bought by Thomas Motors in 1919. Two years later it was converted to a single deck saloon.

The "Scarlet Pimpernel" seen here at the Barry Hotel was used on the first regular advertised service to Cardiff. Started by Barry Motors in July 1920, the fare was 2s. 3d. (11p).

"Long before White's, Thompson's or anybody....my dad had two buses......one was called the Violet and the other one was the Silver King and it was only 1d and 2d to ride then. And I used to take the money and they wouldn't give it to me, because they said I wasn't old enough and I was disgusted because I was 15 - I'm gone 90 now - I'm the only one that's left out of the whole lot of us."

Elizabeth Sharman

Fred Robinson and his son, Walter, c. 1912/13

"When people travelled by train, they'd arrive at either Barry Dock or Barry station. At Barry station, there was a man, Mr. Purcell, who was the agent for delivering your parcels and he would collect your parcels.....and he would deliver to your house. Now up at Barry Dock and Cadoxton, the agent was F.C. Robinson and he did exactly the same. He would collect luggage and deliver it to your house and on the same principle he would go to your house to collect luggage to take to the station if you were going on holiday."
Jack Stevens

"........at 14 years of age, I went to work for a well known baker in the town, Walter Tamlyn, who had a bakery in Station Street, and a very famous baker's van known as a Jowett. It was only two cylinders so it meant that when you went out on a bread round you couldn't get anywhere near the top of Barry until you were half empty."

George Storey

A.D.C. coach owned by Reliance Motors, Barry, 1928

41

The first shops in Barry, Priory Hill, 1890's

Harry Press, "Fruiterer and Fishmonger"

F.J. Greener: "A good selection of up-to-date articles suitable as presents at reasonable prices"; 118 Holton Road, ("opposite Tynewydd Road, where the Brakes start for the Island)", Barry Dock

"We had a shop on the corner of our street. It was called Mill's shop and if you didn't have any money she'd say, 'Well, pay next week'. What if you haven't got it next week? 'Well, forget about it.' And that's how they were!"
Elizabeth Sharman

W.J. Cousins, 79 Main Street, 1914. Cousins came to Barry from Somerset at the turn of the century. These are his four children.

Thomas Trought, 16 Broad Street, c. 1904

"I was one of six girls .....Hand me downs! I used to cry sometimes when I had to wear something belonging to my sister older than me, you know. And I used to cry because my mother used to buy new things for the older ones, and the young ones were passed on."
Phyllis John

Harvey St, c. 1905

"My mother kept a cane. She didn't use it.....they were strict when you were at the table. You weren't to chat, just to get on with your food. One of my sisters, she was a little devil, she'd do what she wanted to, she was a bit headstrong. And my mother used to take the cane down, hang it over the edge of the table and say, 'Now get on with your meal, otherwise you'll feel a taste of this.' That was enough, mind."
Phyllis John

"We had to go to live in rooms. You couldn't have a house, you couldn't afford it. And I had 2 rooms - a bedroom and a downstairs room. Cost me seven shillings a week rent."
Elsie Phipps

The Golden Steps, Porthkerry, Barry.

"Most of the people in that area would have someone at sea, and they would go and not come back and there would be no-one to bury.....This was very much like a mining village where you supported one another."
Maureen Flipse

47

". . . . . everybody gave something . . ."

"The amount of coal exported from Barry Dock continued to increase until 1913 and in that year, almost 11½ million tons were exported."

Leonard Davies

Dan Davies (far left), Jim's father, with three other soldiers, signed and dated "5/1/19"

"I can remember soon after war broke out in 1914, that my mother took me and my sister, in one of these big baby carriages all the way from near Central Park, Barry, to Whitmore Bay .....we walked both ways, you couldn't take these big carriages on the bus. And we took our tea and went to the western end and I can remember we had banana sandwiches. After tea, we were all startled on the beach by the fort firing a shell. It came out of the blue and when we looked out to sea we saw a ship going along Whitmore Bay and it suddenly then turned at right angles and then turned right again at right angles, to go along Whitmore Bay and as it was going along the Bay, I can remember seeing a man waving a flag. It was a blue flag, which I believe was the Greek flag and this time no shell was fired.

My mother boiled the tea with a little sort of oil burner. It was round with a sort of mesh and she used methylated spirits and there was a sort of tripod attached to it and you put the kettle on that."

Iorwerth Prothero

"During the war, Barry was used as an embarkation point for sending the troops abroad, especially France. Of course, Barry sent an enormous amount of coal to France too. You must remember that in the First World War, the German army over-ran the coal areas of France around Arras and N.E. France. The result was, for the rest of the war, we had to supply all France's civilian needs, industrial needs and our own army and keep France going. If it hand't been for us, France would have gone under. Barry sent an enormous amount of coal and a lot of troops went out there too, and, of course, we were fighting all over the world. Coal and troops had to go all over the world.

Now they used to stay at the Drill Hall, bottom of Gladstone Road where Mr. Fouracre has his undertaker's business ....they stayed one night or two and the next day they would go off onto the ship and over to France."

Iorwerth Prothero

"To protect Barry from the aeroplanes coming over, to hide it if you like, they had these smokescreens. And during the daytime they were parked on the perimeters of Barry. And one favourite place was all along Romilly Park. They'd be nose to nose, all these smokescreens, ready to go, as it began to be dusk. And as it got dark, they'd go off and stop at appointed places all around the town. And one stopped just outside the door of my house where I'm living at the present moment. They'd start the engines going and these engines pumped oil onto a hot plate, I suppose, which vapourised. And this black smoke came off, so you couldn't see a thing. But not only did it go up, it came in all the houses. We had to shut our doors, to shut our windows, and the smell that came inside......And it used to permeate and stink the house out. You'd cough terrible, you couldn't do anything about it, and this used to be a regular thing, night after night, when there was an air raid on."

Jack Stevens

Upper Holton Road, early 1900's

"Now I can remember a food queue during the war, now this would be about 1917, when food rationing came in....there was a branch of the Maypole Company opposite the jewellers next to the Vic in Lower Holton Road....And I can still see a queue of women four feet deep, stretching from the Maypole down to Thompson Street and then right the way down Thompson Street almost to the lowest part and they would be four abreast and they all had these rush baskets."

Iorwerth Prothero

"Sometimes you'd find yourself at the end there, and just as you'd got up to Holton Road, the word would be passed around, 'Sold Out. No more'. And you wouldn't get any, only the lucky ones who were up at the front. And I can remember on one occasion getting on a bike and riding to Penarth, because we heard there was some butter going in the Penarth Maypole. And I brought some butter back from Penarth. It was very difficult in those days. Not like the last war - at least you had rations then. But it wasn't like that in the first war."

Jack Stevens

"We celebrated, in 1919, the armistice on the eleventh day of the eleventh month at the eleventh hour - 11 o' clock in the morning, eleventh month, November, and the eleventh day. And always at 11 o'clock dead on. Everything stopped still. The first twelve months of the armistice after the end of the war, everyone would reverence that particular time because .....everybody was grieving over loved ones who had died in the war and naturally two or three minutes silence was a big thing. We wanted to see more of it, so we asked the caretaker of the office could we go up on the clock tower. On the clock of the office there's a big space and we used to sit up there against the clock and we could see everything on the Dock itself. At 11 o'clock everything stopped - the trucks, bump, bump, bump, dead stop, the cars of the road stopped, the workmen standing to attention, right across the Dock on the general cargo side, the dockers they stopped. But one man didn't. He walks along the quay wall and apparently he said to his mate, 'You're all bloody fools,' and he went on walking to what he was doing.....And suddenly the hooters go again, end of the 2 minutes silence. One man turned around, he just picks up this man by the collar, another catches hold of his feet, just swings him and straight into the dock, and said, 'Next time, you stop too!' "

David Wiltshire

"......the coal trade gradually went down and down and down. Well, then the mines were on short time and the coal companies wanted the wages to be cut down...of course, it culminated in the big strike of 1926. Now, miners will say it wasn't a strike but they were locked out, and to a certain extent it was quite true because when the trade union, turned up for a vital conference they were told that Stanley Baldwin had gone to bed and his valet refused to wake him."

Iorwerth Prothero

"In 1926, the S.S. Valesia, laden with coal, ran aground on Friar's Point. She broke in half and beached on the sand. The coal was transferred to boats, although people helped themselves to a lot of it!"

Jack Stevens

"It was terrible....it really was poverty, you know. We had a place where we used to go in the school hall....and have dinners, and wonderful dinners they were too, you know, because everybody gave something, and the ladies would cook for us - pots of stew and you know, things like that, nothing elaborate - roast this and roast that - but a big pot of stew, pot of soup, you know. It was really lovely. I'd rather those days than today, 'cos they couldn't care a button about you......"
Elizabeth Sharman

"Since most people worked by day, the political meetings were held in the evening. There would be long speeches, they would be listened to attentively, there would be heckling and at the end there would be questions, but the square would be crammed full of people for ordinary political speeches. Nowadays, I don't suppose even a cabinet minister would fill that square."
Iorwerth Prothero

Holton Road and Kings Square, early 1900's

"I don't remember the 1926 strike - I was more concerned with boys at the age of 16."
Phyllis Caldwell

BARRY AND DISTRICT
Ratepayers and Property Owners' Association.

DON'T SPEND £125,000
OF YOUR MONEY ON
OLD LIGHTS & OLD METHODS
BUT BE UP TO DATE AT
HALF THE COST!

A GREAT
PUBLIC MEETING
at the **WESLEY HALL**, Holton Rd.
ON WEDNESDAY DEC. 7TH
AT 7.30 P.M.

☞ **COME in CROWDS** ☜
AND HELP SWITCH ON THE CURRENT FOR
ELECTRICITY
IN BARRY!

"BARRY HERALD."

"Electricity was used for the Docks buildings from the earliest time, so the Docks always had electricity. The first use of electricity outside the Docks in Barry was on December 22, 1896, the Windsor Hotel in Holton Road. They were the first people. Now in the home, it didn't come in until the 1920's."

Barry Castle 1895.
G.D. Kilcatt

"There was a butcher. He specialised in being a ship's butcher. Well, he sent his assistant down one day with his son to the Dock to deliver meat to a ship and they tied the horse and cart up to a bollard at the southern end of the old Dock ......and his assistant went off with a big bag of meat and the boy stayed there, looking after the horse. Well, after a bit, the assistant came back with a basket and he said, 'Eh, this ship has got electricity. Come along and have a look at it.' And so, young Burnett left the horse tied to the bollard and went to the ship. Now when they were away there was a certain amount of shunting going on ....chu chu chuchuchuchu ... and the poor thing was so startled it jumped straight forward into the Dock and there the weight of the cart carried the poor thing down and it was drowned. Well, when young Burnett went to tell his father, his father lost his temper and thumped him, gave him a good thumping. Well, a couple of days later, the dock manager wrote to Mr. Burnett and said, 'I understand, Mr. Burnett, that the horse and cart which fell down into the dock the other day belonged to you. Will you kindly take steps to have it removed at once?' So the old man had to hire a tug, put the carcass on, take it out to sea and throw it overboard and this was done. And when the bill came in, he thumped his son again. After a few days, Mr. Burnett got a letter from the Cardiff Rural District Council. 'Dear Mr. Burnett, a horse carcass has been washed up on Rhoose beach. We understand that it probably is yours. Will you, therefore, take steps to have it removed from the beach at once?' So Burnett had to go down to a farmer in Rhoose and ask him to supply a cart and load the cart with the horse's carcass, take it to a field, dig a hole and bury the horse. And when the bill from that came along to Mr. Burnett, he thumped his son again."

Iorwerth Prothero

"If you're talking about the '30's and '40's, it was before there was a welfare state so life was different and I don't think you can compare it with today. In those days, if you didn't have money, you didn't have money."

Maureen Flipse

Holton Road, 1910

"In the '30's, the world went protection mad ....tariffs and protection ... and an enormous number of countries in the '30's, they ran for cover ... countries began to pass acts to protect their own industries which meant putting duties on goods and in many cases British coal had a higher duty put on than before."

Iorwerth Prothero

"I noticed we seemed to have a great number of soups. We ate a great deal of soup and I can remember I used to love butter and I still love butter with bread when I'm drinking soup and my contribution was to have one thick hunk of bread without butter. That was my contribution to the effort during the great strike.

.....there were thousands of people who (were) really very badly off, very badly off .....it's the people who depended on coal and shipping, they're the people who suffered at the ports. The boilermakers went through a bad time, the tippers, the coal trimmers and, of course, all the unskilled labourers and people like that. There was enormous poverty in Barry."

Iorwerth Prothero

"And if you look back to 1934, things were very difficult, it was difficult to get a job, and I couldn't really see any future. So instead of going to school, one Monday morning I went down to the Pier Head and jumped on a ship. I was fourteen and a quarter then, and I went to sea. And my father, my family, never knew where I was."

Dai Woodham

59

"In 1939, after war broke out, I belonged to the Saint John's Ambulance Brigade and we used to meet up at Gladstone School. And Dr. Thomas, who was the Medical Officer of Health, and was in charge of ARP (Air Raid Precaution) during the war, he had to suddenly staff depots, to be used as hospitals and first-aid parties. And, of course, he came up to us in St. John's to find people to staff them and I was asked if I would be the leader in charge of the first aid parties at High Street School, and all the time I was there I kept my own log-book of events and a lot of these pictures are pictures that I took actually while we were practising."

Jack Stevens

"I remember the day the war started because I was going down the shop from my house in Jenner Road and it was a beautiful day and I remember a friend of mine stopped me saying, 'There's a war on', and I remember saying, 'Is there?' and that was it.

But the worst I remember about the war from a personal point of view, I think, was the smoke screens ...To put off the German bombers, especially on a very fine moonlit night, they had an arrangement all along the pavements of the roads of paraffin lamps, which they used to light and all it gave off a sickly smoke, which, of course, was drifted into the air and covered the town .... to stop the bombers seeing it, and every time they lit them I was virtually sick ....'

George Storey

"I went to school one morning and I was late ....I was mitching prayers and I went around the back of the school and sat on the steps. And as I was doing so, out of the cloudy sky came a German bomber and dropped his bombs on the Docks obviously trying for the oil tanks on the Mole at the west end of No. 1 Dock. He missed but I don't think I've ever been so frightened in my life when I saw it."

George Storey

"When stuff was on rations, any stuff that came in, these railwaymen would tip their wives off. 'Tell your mates get there early', they'd say when it was being delivered. So that's what we used to do. We'd go out queuing early in the morning and there was a shop in Dock View Road, Jeffries and Rich, and they used to supply the ships with stuff. So now we had a tip that he had treacle in, but we had to take our own basins to have it put in. So, of course, here we goes. We're all down there early in the morning. But it was black treacle and our Mam made us suet pudding for tea. Oh, my God. I couldn't eat it."

Elsie Phipps

"I was the air-raid warden for the Docks ....Whenever the siren went, everybody had to be on post, and one particular day, the planes came over quite near. You could hear the guns going off. The general office itself was the headquarters of all information, anything happening, any part of the Dock. I was on that night and the two watchers alongside of me. I suddenly missed them. 'Where's the fire-watchers gone, now?' 'Oh, they've gone outside'. 'Ah,' I said, 'they've left the doors open.' 'So', I said, 'I'll go and see where they've got to.' They'd gone out, left the swing doors open. And I go out now to find where they are. As I got back

to the swing doors, all I got was the swing doors coming back and a big furnace of heat hitting me in the face .... I spun round in the hall, back and forth and finally landed back in the office. I saw the thing drop, I never heard it. All I had was a blast of flame .....heat...."

David Wiltshire

"There were a couple of houses actually bombed in Barry. One was in Oxford Street, and my friend lived there. She had shrapnel in her leg and it was terribly exciting because she had to be taken to hospital. We were in Lower School having French one day and an enemy plane came and swooped down. And we had a French mistress, and she was terribly precise, and she said, 'Under the desk, girls.' And we all went under the desks, and the plane went zooming around over the docks, and we thought awful things were going to happen. And all that happened funnily enough was that he dropped a gun, a hand gun, over the docks, and went away. I can remember seeing Cardiff in flames. I was up in the window and you could see the horizon all red. Cardiff was

burning.
We used to see wrecks. One was right at the beginning of the war, and the harbour was full of oranges and lemons and grapefruit. We all went down, trying to find something without oil on it, but we didn't succeed.
I can remember the first time American soldiers came - for a funny reason really because our soldiers had big boots, and when you heard them marching, you heard the clumping. And all of a sudden we saw these people - they didn't have rough uniforms like our lads, they were much smoother - and you couldn't hear them; they were wearing crepe soles.
And, of course, we'd never seen any black people - and there were whole regiments of coloured soldiers came over here and that was a surprise to us children."
Mary Thomas

ORANGES

So many of them among the stones,
each like a float over a lobster pot
coming in numerous as the drowned.

Up early at the Little Harbour,
we found the treasure we'd sought
all the Saturdays of childhood.
First gold brought generously
to a mean Britain. I remember
the water calm as milk licking
the sand with little oily tongues.

We filled our sleeves,
gathered our skirts to make sacks,
bumped uncomfortable homeward.
Crates like the smashed ribcages of sheep.
Across milky water the wreck
was langorous, her tilted deck
rolling with Atlanta's gold.

Salt at first bite, then bitter pith
and a sharp juice. My tongue searched
for the cloying concentrate I knew
or the scent the miner spoke of,
and orange broken at snap-time underground
breathed a mile away
if the wind's in the right direction.
Gillian Clarke

April 15th, 1989

"The Geest Line came to Barry in 1957, the subsequent import trade in bananas from the West Indies and return cargoes of general cargo accounting for approximately 30% of trade. In April 1986, ABP inaugurated a new Multi-million pound facility named the Windward Terminal, designed to meet Geest's requirements. It is now generally recognised as one of the best fruit-handling facilities in Europe."

ABP

HOME FRONT

That winter of our Island Fortress,
the docks blacked-out and sirens wailing,
the house closed its brittle silence around her.
Rain drummed the windows behind her children's dreams.
Over the months she saved from her widow's pay
and the hours of cleaning at the manse
seven silver coins, one from the abdication year
with the head of the love-lost king.

Should the coastline be split by incoming shells,
parachutes flower in the Vale
and jackboots strut in King's Square,
then she would lay her six children
to sleep, sealing the windows and doors
with newspapers and blankets.
Seven shillings' worth of gas
would deliver them out of occupation.

For months she has dreamt of his lost freighter,
torpedoed six days out of New York,
men overboard, gagging on salt and diesel.
How the ship reared and plunged like a whale,
her wash sweeping cold hands from flotsam.
As he sank into the anonymous dark
the final waves from her
minting coins from the constant moon.

Tonight the City of London burns
with St Paul's untouched at the very centre.
At the edge of night the Welsh ports sound no alarms.
She opens the curtains to a moon-bright sky,
counts out the coins in the tea-caddy
and holds them, cupped in her palms.
OMN. REX. Defender of the Faith. Emperor of India.
The seven polished shillings sing in her hands.
Tony Curtis

"I remember hiding in the cupboard under the stairs when they used to go over, when the bombers used to go over. They used to pass right over, we were terrified. My husband was in Burma for four and a half years. My youngest boy didn't know him at all. He was a baby when he left – six months old. When he came back, he was going to school. So he had to get to know his father."

Phyllis John

"The biggest trade we had was with France and Ireland -boats were coming over weekly from France and Ireland and in and out. Well, now when the war finished, France had a load of coal from Germany. Germany was repaying their debts to France by giving them coal. The result was you lost all the trade from France .....And that's when your trade started to diminish. It's never recovered since."
David Wiltshire

"The Engine Graveyard", Barry

"When I first loaded ships, cargoes of scrap for export in 1958, the whole thing was hand-baled. Everything had to be handled by hand. We needed X number of men, and needed all sorts of help, it was a terribly tough job. Now when I load a ship, I don't need a single man, I don't need one man at all, a) because the ships are constructed differently, and b) because we use different mechanised means; we use grabs which can operate and put it in place. So we don't actually need a single man, and that's the difference."

Dai Woodham

"Barry never supplied enough work for its children, its sons and its daughters."
Iorwerth Prothero

Barry Dock Centenary No1 Liberty Shi

68

Joe, E. Mann leaves Barry 1947.

Leon Vint's Electric Palace Concert Party

4

*"That's it, that's it,
That's how life should be."*

"Vint's, Thompson Street - originally it was the only place in Barry where they used to have turns and they'd show films. The first talking films were shown in this place. It was opened in 1910, built on the site of the old Salvation Army Hall.

Leon Vint, that was his stage name, his real name was William Moores.

The famous singer, Isabel Bailey, was at one time a member of Vint's choir."

Jack Stevens

Bindles, 1950

72

"We went to the cinema quite a lot; it used to be we'd go on a Saturday and also on a Wednesday, and that was usually quite regular. Apart from that, we played hockey and different games. And we went down to the bottom gate at the girls' school to meet the boys lunchtime. Things don't change, do they?"

Mary Thomas

Barry Railway Company Servants Orphanage Fund Concert, Old Romilly Hall (previously a Market Hall), Broad Street, pre 1914

TRAVIS STREET

CORONATION FESTIVITIES

Commencing 3 p.m. on June 2nd, 1953

"GOD SAVE THE QUEEN"

ADRIAAN FLIPSE

Victoria Park, Cadoxton

"The bowling green produced one international at least in Eddie Thompson who died somewhere round 1960. His two sons still live in Barry, now retired and both of them play for Barry Central Bowling Club.

I can remember Eddie Thompson, boys hero-worshipped him. He was such a kind man and always recognised us, he'd always speak to us in the street ...."
Iorwerth Prothero

"The stakes for Barry Town against Swansea were a place in Europe against possibly some of the best sides in the world and a lot of people thought we were going to win the game ....so did I! We didn't take our chances and possibly that cost us the result ....maybe next season."
Ashley Griffiths, Captain, Barry Town Football Club

"My uncle, George Barker, he and a chap in the Royal Hotel, Griffiths, started up with some men the Barry Town Football Club. They didn't have many funds so he went to Plymouth for the jerseys for the boys, the Barry team ... He begged and pleaded for the Plymouth jerseys, the old ones. And they gave him all the red jerseys, and he brought them back to Barry and they were all red. Well somehow or other, through the years, they've changed to green. But the first colour for Barry was red."
Phyllis Caldwell

'When we were children in Abingdon Street .....there was no danger then, not like there is now, no cars, 'cos it was only a one-way street. And we used to play all sorts of games - 'Across the Stream' as we used to call it. One would stand in the middle of the street and the others would all run in a crowd across and if the one in the middle could catch the one, they had to stand in the middle. Then we used to play 'The wind, the wind, the wind blows high, the rain comes scattering from the sky.' All in a ring. And the one in the middle would say -'She is handsome, she is pretty, she's a girl from London City', and then they'd say -'Who goes courting 1,2,3 Tell me who is she?'.... and the one in the middle catches hold of one of the children, you know, their friends usually, they go in the middle with them, until there's hardly .... enough to go round. .... we had whip and top. Kiddies don't play that now. The boys played marbles, the girls didn't. And there were lots of games we made up.''

Phyllis Caldwell

"...... we'd go down Lombard Street..... there was a woman very stout and she had a devil of a job waddling about and she had a shop in the front room and we'd go and ring the door bell. The poor old soul would come running out, best way she could, and we'd be gone! Then at the bottom in Holton Road, there was an outfitters -more like working clothes. They always had a couple of chairs outside with bundles of trousers ...... postmen's and all that ..... they'd finished with. These trades people would buy them and put them for sale for the people that done the dirty work on the docks, the navvies and all that .... and they always had big labels on them, the price of them. And we used to pick them off and tear them up. And on the corner of Thompson Street was Hicks', the Chemist. They had a bell on their side door so we'd run there, ring the bell, run farther down Thompson Street. The wine shop would be there, Owen, I can remember that and we'd ring there and they'd come out shouting and swearing at us but they never touched us, you know. And then across from there was a Chinese laundry, and we were convinced -you know kids get funny ideas - we were sure that they were smoking opium and we wanted to see them. Well, the inside of their windows were painted with white paint and some of it had started to come off. So anyhow, I, like the others, I go and have a look. I put my eye to the space to see. We'd see them ironing and all, but we never seen what we expected to see ...the opium den. So anyhow, this one day, we went down there as usual and I'm the first. 'Go on Elsie', they say, and I puts my eye to the window and as I puts my eye to this hole in the window so there's another eye level with mine. That cured me. I was frightened to death.''

Elsie Phipps

"And all through the summer we never missed going out with the children. We used to start Easter. On the Sunday, we'd go down Porthkerry picking primroses. On Easter Monday, we'd go to the fairground and spend more than we could really afford, but that would be their only trip to the fairground for the summer. Then, the next week, it'd be violets we'd be after, then cowslips and then we used to have those wild irises, those tall ones, pick those. Then it'd be time to go picking blackberries and mushrooms and watercress and we used to go out and pick it all. We never bought anything like that. And then about September picking hazelnuts to put away for Christmas.''

Elsie Phipps

"The people who came on holiday from the Valleys and from the Midlands and I think there was a recognition that the people who came from Birmingham came for one day in the year - that was their holiday - and they were working class like the rest of us that used the beaches within walking distance, and there was a kind of affinity .... they were all the same, a bus load of people from the Valleys were just ordinary like the rest of us and there wasn't a conflict."
Maureen Flipse

"The Welsh Lido"

Beach donkeys, Barry Island, 1905

"Barry Island .. it was one stretch of sand, and bagged down with sand bags were tiny, tiny roundabouts on the sand. And, of course, I never had any money because my mother wasn't all that well off at that time. And I used to stand and watch the kids on the roundabouts - only a penny a ride. And if I could, I'd sneak on, but that wasn't very often. They were too watchful .... they were good days, you know, no evil about like there is now ....."

Phyllis Caldwell

Watch Tower Bay – Annual Regatta – 1920's

Let's go to Barry Island, Maggie fach,
And give all the kids one day by the sea,
And sherbet and buns and paper hats,
And a rattling ride on the Figure eight;
We'll have tea on the sands, and rides on the donkeys,
And sit in the evening with the folk of Cwm Rhondda,
Singing the sweet old hymns of Pantycelyn
When the sun goes down beyond the rocky islands.
Come on, Maggie fach, or the train will be gone
Then the kids will be howling at home all day,
Sticky with dirt and gooseberry jam.
Leave the washing alone for today, Maggie fach,
And put on your best and come out to the sun
And down to the holiday sea.
We'll carry the sandwiches in a big brown bag
And leave our troubles behind for a day
With the chickens and the big black tips
And the rival soup-kitchens, quarrelling like hell.
Come, Maggie fach, with a rose on your breast
And an old Welsh tune on your little red lips,
And we'll all sing together in the Cardiff train
Down to the holiday sea.

Idris Davies (from the 'The Angry Summer')

"This is the first Figure 8 which was over at Barry Island. When this picture was taken, it was the only building on the whole piece of ground there –it was nothing but very coarse grass and sand. And the engine that used to drive that was a gas engine, and it used to be in the shed at the bottom of the tower, with a great clanking chain."

Jack Stevens

Figure 8 Railway, Barry Island

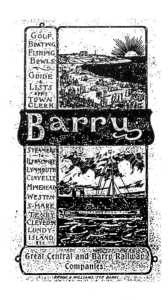

"I remember these little paddle steamers going out to Minehead across the water to Weston, Ilfracombe, and also going out for day trips in the summer - Campbell's they were called. I went to Weston, it cost 5s or 6s, which was a lot of money then, because wages for a labourer were about 30s a week. I remember walking down the tunnel; that tunnel seemed a long, long way down when you were a kid. And over in Weston, you went out on the long pier. I got sunburnt the first time I went there."

Iorwerth Williams

"What do you do when you've saved up for twelve months and it's your day out - you're going to make the most of it, aren't you, whatever the weather, whatever the conditions, then go back and say, 'We had a wonderful time,' which they did. People in the Valleys remember their childhood and their visits to Barry Island with the church outing or with the miners' gala."

Maureen Flipse

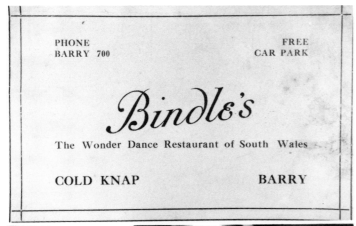

PHONE
BARRY 700

FREE
CAR PARK

Bindle's

The Wonder Dance Restaurant of South Wales

COLD KNAP

BARRY

Part of Cafe & Ballroom, Bindle's Cold Knap Barry

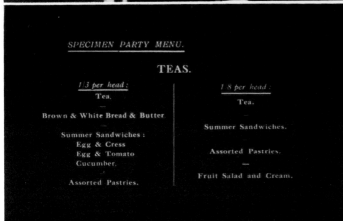

SPECIMEN PARTY MENU.

TEAS.

1/3 per head :
Tea.

Brown & White Bread & Butter.

Summer Sandwiches :
Egg & Cress
Egg & Tomato
Cucumber.

Assorted Pastries.

1/8 per head :
Tea.

Summer Sandwiches.

Assorted Pastries.

Fruit Salad and Cream.

BARRY ISLAND
Between the Haunted House,
The sea-blue wall of the Big Dipper,
The fruit machines, the trinket stall,
And the sea,

Going round and round,
Its horses on poles ascending and descending,
Yellow and red,
Words circulating round its roof
Reading: *Here are*
the ever popular
stand of galloping
horses and flying birds
patronised and enjoyed
by all classes.

Stand, circulating,
Poised, clear—
All classes—
That's it, that's it,
That's how life should be.

John Idris Jones

Dock No. 1, April 24, 1989

5

".....this drawing from memory of lines, where, steely-silver, what we are now touches everything that made us ....."

"I started up in the office in the engineer's department. I worked there for 49 years. I was sitting in the house one day. My niece knocked at the door and said, 'Come on quick, the office is on fire.' And she took me up in the car to Dock View Road and I stood out and watched it and I tell you I almost cried ....."
Jack Stevens

Docks Office fire, Saturday 3 March, 1984. The building was re-opened by Mr. Wyn Roberts, M.P., on 29th April, 1986, after extensive restoration.

"People in places like Barry had to fight for what they've got .... to keep it."

Phyllis John

"What I see the difference in the present day .... if you've got clothes that you've finished with, and you want to get rid of them, there's not many people will accept a gift of a second-hand dress ..... and yet when I was younger, we were glad if someone passed something over ..... they don't do it so much now. It's different. You've got to have new and you've got to have the latest."

Elsie Phipps

"The community, it's a family isn't it? There everybody knew everyone else and knew what their role was and trusted them, trusted them. I don't know who you can trust in your house these days.'

'people did support one another in every kind of way - illness, births, deaths - it was your neighbours that came and helped out ....."

Maureen Flipse

"if they had anything, you could have half ....."
Elizabeth Sharman

Dock No. 2, February 1, 1989

LINES AT BARRY

Morning light steely and sharp on the docks-water
and beyond, outlining a ship in the grey Channel.
At berth, one banana ship white against the old mill
        building
where, you say, a forest of masts grew in the sun,
filling your great-grandfather's vision
as he rounded Friar's Point.

Ten days rowing from Fishguard
the length of South Wales. 1898.
Your grandmother lived her first week
in that small boat as they hugged the shore,
sheltering each night where lights marked
fire and food and life.

This is not a unique story:
each dip of his creaking blades pulling
towards coal, English and the new century.

Twenty years on he was carpenter to the town,
settled and secure in his middle life.
They'd worked all night to build a platform
for the notables, under the Stars and Stripes,
the Red Dragon, the Union Jack.
The next day he took his place in the crowd
around King's Square and stretched for a view.
This is where the Yanks first came in,
eight days rolled across the ocean
then marched in columns up from the packed, grey
        harbour.
The doughboys formed in dress order,
spreading and flexing their sea-legs,
the men bound in puttees, their officers' boots glowing,
the strange, stiff-brimmed campaign hats,
lines of polished Springfields raised against the Kaiser.

And for a moment between the speeches,
the cheering, the singing and the drill,
for a moment the lines were still and erect
as those distant masts had been for a moment still,
when the only sound was the sound of the tide pulling
his tiny boat: he saw again Sarah's tired smile,
the baby pressed to her nipple and sucking,
sucking hard, as if nothing else, not even he,
existed.

As this new morning goes, the haze
lifts slowly from the Channel, unveils
the munitions ship with her red flags up
and lighters packed with shells
drawing lines of foam to the smack centre of her sides.

Three lifetimes, two wars running to this moment—
and none of this is unique, this telling,
this drawing from memory of lines
where, steely-silver, what we are now
touches everything that made us,
and is dangerous, and shines.
            Tony Curtis

"The value of the Docks itself, the culture it provided, this wonderful mixed culture - there are people living on estates who probably don't know that their family originally came from another country ..... they don't know.
Some people will wonder, why didn't we ever know any of this happened, how important the Docks were to Barry. Your future's based on your past, anyway, and it is important to know these things, it really is. It isn't every town that has such a background."

Maureen Flipse

Valley and Vale gratefully acknowledges the financial assistance of South East Wales Arts Association, Ogwr Borough Council, the Margaret and Gwendoline Davies Charities, the Welsh Arts Council, South Glamorgan County Council, Vale of Glamorgan Borough Council, Barry Town Council and the valuable support of local community organisation.

Elvis '56

In November 1955 Elvis Presley was signed to RCA Victor from Sun Records, a small independent firm based in Memphis. Up to that time, five of his singles had been released. None had reached the national Pop charts.

On January 10, 1956, "Heartbreak Hotel" was recorded at the RCA studio in Nashville, but it wasn't until the end of February that the single appeared on *Billboard's* Top 100.

On the evening of January 28 Elvis debuted on national television on the Dorsey Brothers' "Stage Show," the first of six appearances. He was just twenty-one years old.

Foreword

If Elvis Presley hadn't died, this book might not have been published. Within twenty-four hours after his death on August 16, 1977, people I'd never heard of phoned me, asking for my photographs of Elvis taken at the beginning of his career.

My collection of over 3,800 negatives of Elvis had been resting in the company of thousands of other negatives, all locked tight in unmarked boxes in a corner of my cellar for over twenty years. Not until I had an opportunity to see all the publications churned out after his death did I suspect how unique my photographs were. Most of the pictures that had been published were public photos—Elvis on stage, at an airport, leaving a car, or publicity poses produced by Hollywood and the record business. There seemed to be very little material that was natural and personal.

I believed an opaque curtain had been lowered around Elvis sometime during the period of his first appearance on the "Ed Sullivan Show" in September of 1956.

After attending several Elvis conventions and seeing even more photographic material that appeared after his death, my belief in the curtain became conviction.

I recently visited Anne Fulchino, Head of Pop Publicity at RCA Victor from 1954 to 1960, for the first time in twenty years. She told me that the publicity files assembled on Elvis at RCA had been given to the Colonel at his request in the fall of 1956. From that point on, the Colonel controlled all media access to the private Elvis.

The only conclusion I could draw about my photographs was that they were probably the first and the last look at the day-to-day life of Elvis Presley.

I was asked and also tempted at times to come out with a quick book, but in thinking about Elvis' thoroughly professional manner toward his music, I felt this book deserved the best I could give. It has taken me over a year to do so.

People ask me, what was Elvis really like? To me, he was an enigma. I was close and yet I can't pretend to say I knew him. I was just his shadow for a short period of time at the beginning of his career. I was not a friend, really; I was a reporter whose pen was a camera.

Alfred Wertheimer

New York City, June, 1979.

Elvis '56
In the Beginning

Photographs by Alfred Wertheimer
Text by Alfred Wertheimer
and
Gregory Martinelli

COLLIER BOOKS
A Division of Macmillan Publishing Co., Inc.

To my mother, Katy Wertheimer,
I dedicate this book with love.

Acknowledgments:
I would like to thank the following people whose contributions were essential to the completion of this book: Sue Bailey, my right hand on this project, for her dedication to detail; Will Hopkins and his associates, for the design of the book; Charlie Reiche and Ira Mandelbaum of Scope Associates, for their master touch in printing the photographs from the original negatives; Jack Avedisian of Evans-Avedisian Color Lab, Inc., for his fine supervision in making the dye transfer for the cover; Pat Kranish, for critical advice; Anne Fulchino, for giving me the assignment to cover Elvis; Greg Martinelli, for his patience and help in preparing the text; Tennyson Schad, for his advice and counsel; Thérèse Schevtchenko, for her encouragement and understanding; Bob Franchi, Jeff Griffin, and Andy Bryan, for taking care of business at Cinergy; Paul Schutzer, for his prophetic insight about Elvis in '56; Toni Lopopolo, my editor at Macmillan; Colonel Thomas A. Parker, for being one of the more colorful characters I've ever met; Billy Smith, Sean Shaver, Phil Gelormine, Betty Statler, Karen Mullarkey, Robert Pledge, John Durniak, Stuart Gross, John Zap, Ed Pieratt, Monica Ambrose, Lillian D'Agostino, Heidi and Pamela, and Elvis' loyal fans, for their interest which encouraged me to undertake this project; and of course, Elvis, for letting me get so close.

Designed by Will Hopkins and Ira Friedlander/ Will Hopkins Group
Design Assistant Ingrid Von Werz

Copyright © 1979 by Alfred Wertheimer

Macmillan Publishing Co., Inc.
866 Third Avenue, New York, N.Y. 10022
Collier Macmillan Canada, Ltd.
LC No.: 79-3261   ISBN 0-02-061900-6
12 11 10 9 8 7 6 5 4 3 2
Printed in the United States of America
Compositor: CountyPhotoCompositingCorp.
Printer: Halliday Lithograph

Contents

Just Another Assignment

"We have another song here, friends, that, uh, we hope you like … it's called 'Heartbreak Hotel.'"

It was a Thursday afternoon in March 1956 when the phone rang. Three people answered. We were sharing a back room studio on Seventy-fourth Street under the shadow of the Third Avenue El, an elevated train that clattered through the east side of Manhattan. Paul was sitting at his desk doodling another cartoon, Jerry was shooting cheesecake in the back and I was standing in the darkroom looking at another print of Embrace perfume. Anne Fulchino was on the line. She was the publicist for the Pop Record Division of RCA Victor.

I had been free-lancing for about six months, shooting stories on my own that would eventually be sold to *Life* and *Paris Match,* but I was paying the landlord with the fifty dollars per recording session I was making by photographing people like Arthur Rubinstein, Joel Grey and Julius LaRosa. Anne said they had an exciting young singer and asked if I was available on Saturday, the seventeenth.

I said, "Sure, what's up?"

"His name is Elvis Presley."

"Who?"

"El-vis Pres-ley."

"Never heard of him."

Anne, a diminutive woman with curly blond hair and a methodical pace, led me to a small dressing room at the back of CBS Television Studio 50. The guy I'd never heard of was leaning back in a chair with his feet on the make-up table, sporting argyle socks, silk shantung pants and jacket, black shirt, freshly combed slick brown hair and a sneer. He didn't look much like a star, more like just another backstage guy.

When Anne introduced me a balding jewelry salesman was handing him a diamond ring that could have been seen from the back row of Carnegie Hall. Elvis pulled his feet off the table, leaned on the back of another chair, and in a soft low voice with a mild Southern accent, said simply, "Hi." He returned to his examination of the ring, a diamond-studded horseshoe around a gold horse's head. I took my place behind the camera. The salesman closed the deal.

A stagehand poked his head in the door and told Mr. Presley he was wanted on the phone. Elvis slid the new ring onto his finger, studied himself and his diamonds in the mirror, ran a comb through his hair and left for the call.

Downstairs, stagehands banged sets onto loading platforms, directors shouted instructions, spotlights were turned on and shut off. TV cameras were jockeyed across the stage and the Tommy and Jimmy Dorsey Band played on. The Dorsey Brothers' "Stage Show" was to be televised live across the country at 8:30 P.M.

As Elvis hung up, Anne arrived with a reporter whose questions were as crisp as his crew cut.

"How's it feel to do your fifth nationwide TV performance?"

"It feels good."

"Are you prepared?"

"Yeah, I'm prepared."

"Tell me, why do you move your hips around so much? Are you trying to arouse the girls?"

"That's just the way I sing. I can't sing any other way. I need my whole body."

"But you're the only one who needs his whole body, other singers don't sing that way."

"Well, that's other singers, that's not me."

"You're sure you're not trying to be provocative?"

"What?"

"Provocative, you know, lewd."

"No, I'm not lewd, sir."

He politely excused himself. The sneer I had first seen seemed to have nothing to do with his style: His charm was a soft-spoken sensuality and his manners were those of a well-brought-up young man. It was "yes, ma'am" and "no, sir."

It was time for rehearsal. The musicians — a guitarist, a drummer and a bassist — took their positions at center stage in front of the Dorsey Orchestra. An assistant held up a large posterboard and Jimmy Dorsey announced: "And now, we would like to present an entertainer whose provocative style has kicked off quite a momentum around the country. Here he is, Elvis Presley!"

With his guitar around his neck and his hands swinging free, Elvis strolled out to center stage. The lights dimmed, leaving him in the spot and the Dorseys in the dark.

He strummed his guitar with a single stroke, snapped the beat with his left leg and shouted, "Ah one for the money, ah two for the show" and sang something about blue suede shoes and not to step on them. At the guitarist's solo, he did a little dance on the balls of his feet, somewhere between a backward kick and a bump without the grind. I didn't think much about it.

The next number was about a hotel, a ballad he sang with a rich baritone that didn't seem to have much control. He had a good voice, though, and with some more experience, I figured he could develop into a pretty good singer.

After rehearsal I asked Elvis if I could tag along with him. I wasn't looking for an opportunity to probe. If I asked the wrong question I might lose him. I wasn't a reporter, I was a photographer and tagging along was just fine with me. He didn't mind at all.

It was rush hour at the end of a cold winter day when the two of us crossed Broadway, walking free and easy through the sidewalk crowds making their way home. Times Square didn't see us and didn't care.

At a Hollywood-style haberdasher, Elvis passed by racks of pressed white shirts to stacks of dark shirts in rich colors: blues, purples, blacks. None of them caught his fancy. What attracted his attention was a cluster of 8 x 10 glossies of local personalities which were on the wall by the door, pictures of acrobats and nightclub singers who would fade faster than their prints. I took his photograph.

The Warwick Hotel had been built to celebrate an earlier era, but it was now suffering from fatigue. Dim lights preserved its fading floral carpets and mottled walls. Room 527 wasn't a suite, but a simple spacious room with a large mirror hanging over a studio couch. Elvis flopped down on the couch, grabbed a fistful of letters from a cardboard box and began reading. After finishing each letter he tore it into small pieces. The remains were deposited on the coffee table next to a collection of aspirin, stomach and cold remedies and a copy of *The Loves of Liberace*. This routine continued until he rolled onto the pile of letters on the couch and stared at the ceiling. I asked:

"What do you think of the big city?"

"I don't really care too much for the big city."

"Well, do you feel more comfortable down South, down in Memphis?"

"Yeah, a lot more comfortable. People understand me better down there."

He tore up a few more letters, settled down with a cushion and dozed off. I had never covered a subject who fell asleep in front of my camera, but I had my assignment. I took a few more pictures, and when I sat down in one of the soft, thick chairs, I followed his example.

The buzz of an electric shaver woke me up. Elvis was in the bathroom. I tried to figure out a discreet way to take his picture when I decided upon the direct approach. I asked if I could come in and take some pictures. He said, "Sure, why not?"

With one white towel around his hips and another slung over his shoulder, Elvis elevated wet combing to an art, examining each angle with the scrutiny of a portrait artist. He was the perfect subject for a photographer, unafraid and uncaring, oblivious to the invasion of my camera.

It was show-time. Elvis stood at ease in the wings, his hair wet in place, a white silk tie glowing against his black shirt and dark silk suit. A hatch opened in the stage floor and a microphone appeared as the standby light flashed on the left arch of the stage. The Dorsey Orchestra settled in their seats against the rear wall. Elvis' musicians, dressed in white shirts and dark ties, assumed their positions at the center. I crouched below the proscenium of the stage, while behind me the audience, which seemed to have more than its share of teenaged girls, rustled with a restlessness I thought was caused by the excitement of live television.

"On the air" lit up, the Dorsey Orchestra played the opener and before Jimmy got halfway through his introduction of Elvis, the screaming started — not isolated shrieking but an avalanche of sound that took me completely by surprise. I almost dropped my camera.

With a Cheshire cat's grin on his face, Elvis strutted out to the microphone, his hands swinging free as his guitar bobbled against his body. He strummed his guitar once and silenced the crowd. Then he spread his legs, leaned back and belted out, "Ah one for the money, Ah two for the show, three to get ready, now go, cat, go." And he did, swaying, jumping, rocking around so much I could barely keep him in my frame. I hadn't had this problem during rehearsal, but, then, he hadn't had an audience either.

The screaming came in waves, breaking to the extreme motions of his body with such intensity that the Dorseys' signature at the end was barely heard.

Elvis stopped the frenzy when he spoke with a soft Southern drawl.

"Thank ya very much, ladies and gentlemen. That was my latest RCA escape, uh, release . . . ."

A few people got the joke. The girls just sat there with their mouths open.

"We have another one here, we have another song here, friends, that, uh we hope you like . . . it's called 'Heartbreak Hotel.' "

The chorus burst and died again. He strummed the guitar once, leaned into the rigid microphone and wailed, "Waahl, since my baby left me . . . ." Someone shouted "sing it, boy." He did, unleashing such a convulsive reaction that I thought the ushers were going to have to carry people away. I had never seen anything like it before.

It was March in New York and it was cold. It didn't matter. Within five minutes, a handful of fans at the stagedoor cascaded into an entire rooting section. As Elvis stood coatless against the door signing autographs, the crush of the crowd propelled me to the rear.

A teenaged girl stopped me.
"Are you somebody?"
"Sure, I'm somebody."
"Well, who are you?"
"Right now, I'm Elvis' photographer."
"Oh, can I have your autograph?"
I scribbled on a piece of paper. It was not one of my more legible signatures. She held it up to the light of a streetlamp.
"Who?"
"Al Wertheimer."
"Oh."
She jammed it in her coat pocket and joined the squeeze. I had never seen anything like this before, either.

Listening to advice from a representative of William Morris, the agency that booked Elvis on the Dorsey show.

12

(Preceding page) A jewelry salesman makes a pitch in the dressing room before rehearsal for the Dorsey show.

Elvis did buy a ring, a diamond-studded horseshoe around a gold horse's head.

Elvis falls asleep on his fan mail at the Warwick Hotel, New York City, between rehearsal and the evening performance on "Stage Show."

(Following page) The final touch before he leaves the Warwick for CBS Studio 50 and a national audience.

Make-up for the opening act of "Stage Show." Elvis took care of the hair.

"Blue Suede Shoes" live; Scotty Moore, left, on guitar; D.J. Fontana (partially hidden) on drums; Bill Black, right, on bass.

(Following page) "Heartbreak Hotel" live; it was the first time he sang his hit on the Dorsey show without the back-up of the Dorsey Band.

New York Return

"Mr. Presley ... is a rock and roll variation ... of the hootchy-kootchy."

The next three months brought Sir Thomas Beecham, The Four Lovers (who became the Four Seasons) and Perry Como into my life. For Elvis, there was a number-one single in "Heartbreak Hotel," two appearances on the "Milton Berle Show," a screen test with Paramount producer Hal Wallis and a number-one album that topped a list that included "My Fair Lady," Frank Sinatra, Harry Belafonte and "Carousel."

Elvis' second appearance on the "Milton Berle Show" broke the silence of New York's major television critics. Jack Gould of the *New York Times* decided, "Mr. Presley has no discernible singing ability. ... He is a rock and roll variation of one of the most standard acts in show business: the virtuoso of the hootchy-kootchy."

Jack O'Brien of the *New York Journal American* concurred: "Elvis Presley wiggled and wriggled with such abdominal gyrations that burlesque bombshell Georgia Sothern really deserves equal time to reply in gyrating kind. He can't sing a lick, makes up for vocal shortcomings with the weirdest, and plainly planned, suggestive animation short of an aborigine's mating dance."

During a review of my photo contact sheets at RCA Victor, Anne asked me to cover Elvis on Steve Allen's new TV show. She said that even though Elvis was getting a lot of bad press, he was really a sweet boy. So she wanted some "nice" pictures.

I was never encouraged to use color film to photograph Elvis. Although Anne had confidence that Elvis would make it, other people at RCA didn't think he would last for more than six months. Shooting color was expensive; black and white was all that was necessary.

On Friday morning, June 29, I entered a midtown Manhattan rehearsal studio. I had expected to see an auditorium with spotlights and long black curtains. Instead it was a quiet, spare room that probably had once been a shirt factory, with a clean pine floor and tall windows that lit a white ceiling of filigreed tin. Past the vacant folding chairs, I saw a gaunt figure in a rumpled white suit staring into the street. He had deep-set eyes, a hard etched face and wild curly hair. He was Carroll "Junior" Smith, Elvis' cousin.

In the corner, Elvis sat at the piano, wearing a raw silk suit that would have been large on a heavyweight and a pair of two-toned wing tips you could have seen coming a block away. I crossed the room quietly and lingered at the piano, hoping that Elvis would get up and carry the ball. He didn't leap at the chance. I decided to give him another opportunity.

"Hi, Elvis, remember the Tommy Dorsey show."

He looked up as he continued to press the keys. "Yeah."

"Well, Anne wants me to take some more pictures."

"Sure, go ahead."

I stood there while he played the piano. I couldn't tell if he recognized me or if he was just keeping up his side of the conversation.

I resumed my place behind the lens. Into my frame walked a round fellow in a narrow-brimmed straw hat capped off with a feather, wearing a linen suit, a shirt with horizontal stripes and a loosely knotted tie. In the fingers of his left hand was a cigar butt small enough to be held on a toothpick. He was Colonel Thomas A. Parker, Elvis' personal manager. With him were two agents in Brooks Brothers suits, representatives of the William Morris Agency, the New York firm that was directing Elvis' national appearances.

The Colonel was running the conversation, making points with his cigar, speaking in a voice that had the timbre required of a barker on Broadway and a trace of a Southern accent. The agents listened, contributing their share of occasional nods, while Elvis remained seated at the piano. When introduced he gave an easy smile and said, "Hi." One agent with wire-rimmed glasses and a copy of the *New York Times* expressed surprise at Elvis' playing the piano. Elvis grinned and hit a chord, saying that he was just having some fun.

The Colonel, knowing an opportunity when he saw one, went on about the boy's natural and soon to be realized talents, while the other agent slouched over the piano, casually adjusted his bowtie and stared out the tall windows. To this audience, Elvis sang a spiritual.

A door banged open and conversations rumbled in. Steve Allen had arrived with his entourage, along with his stars, Imogene Coca and Andy Griffith. Everyone exchanged customary greetings and did some posing for the NBC photographer, while the Colonel, Elvis' cousin and the two agents took their seats along the wall.

In two days Steve Allen would broadcast his second national television show. He was scheduled opposite Ed Sullivan's "Toast of the Town," a situation that might qualify as unfair competition in the ratings war, had not NBC's game plan been to load Allen with some high-powered names. With the reaction generated by his appearance on the "Milton Berle Show," Elvis was now high-powered.

The rehearsal was a skit written as a takeoff of the Grand Ole Opry, full of "yippy ky ay" and bits of cornball from the old range. Steve played straight man for Andy and Imogene, who had most of the big punch lines. Elvis had a few lines but he spent most of the time watching the pros go through the motions. I had heard Elvis got his start in 1954 in a country and western radio show called "Louisiana Hayride," and if the laughs were on him, he didn't seem to mind. He was relaxed, courteous and attentive.

A secretary whispered to Steve as they wrapped up the rehearsal. He turned to Elvis, who was studiously flipping back and forth through his script, and said,

"The tailor's here."

Elvis looked up, confused, and replied, "Yes, sir? What about?"

"Remember, you're wearing tails while you're singing to the hound dog."

"Oh, yeah, I remember."

I had no idea what they were talking about. I thought it was going to be just another one of Allen's gags.

Elvis stepped into a broom closet and reappeared in baggy pants and floppy tails. With the same unlit cigar jammed in a corner of his mouth, Colonel Parker stepped forward to make sure his boy got a custom job. After the tailor made his last chalk mark, Elvis turned to the mirror across the room, snapped the lapels and checked his hair, with that half-leer, half-smile that kept me guessing.

The room returned to a chapel-like serenity when the door slammed closed on the last of Allen's group. The Colonel instructed Junior about hotel accommodations and train schedules for a concert in Richmond, Virginia, the following day. Elvis didn't pay any attention. He was back at the piano playing another spiritual.

(Preceding page) He was the first to arrive for the "Steve Allen Show" rehearsal. New York City, June 29, 1956.

(Above) Before Allen arrived, Colonel Thomas A. Parker, right, Elvis' personal manager, chats with two agents from the William Morris Agency, which booked Elvis' national appearances.

Colonel Parker instructs Carroll "Junior" Smith, Elvis' cousin and constant companion, regarding travel arrangements to Richmond, Virginia.

After rehearsal he assists the tailor in fitting Elvis for tails; the outfit was part of Allen's plan for the "new Elvis Presley."

Left to right: Andy Griffith, Imogene Coca, Steve Allen and Elvis rehearse the comedy sketch, "Range Round-up." Elvis' role as "Tumbleweed Presley" was his first acting part on national television.

Richmond

"I like all girls. I like 'em all."

My Friday evening began in the darkroom where I was developing the day's work. I always wanted my photographs to be true, and that was the way I tried to take the picture — simple, natural, unobtrusive. If I could have reduced myself to a fly on the wall I would have, but that kind of a bargain could be made only with the supernatural, so I had to content myself with a tan windbreaker, Clark's crepe-soled shoes and available light. Flashbulbs had to be avoided.

The only place I had covered Elvis was in New York City, north of the Mason–Dixon line and quicker than a cabbie's temper. I wanted to see him on his own turf. I packed my gear and caught the 8:45 P.M. out of Pennsylvania Station.

At 6 A.M. on Saturday, June 30, the Richmond, Fredericksburg and Potomac Railroad let me off in Richmond, capital of the Confederacy and home of the nation's tobacco industry. I hailed a cab, told the driver "Jefferson Hotel" and lit up a Viceroy.

The desk clerk informed me that Elvis hadn't arrived yet, so I hopped back into the cab and told the man to take me back to the train station. The cabbie, a veteran who looked as if he'd been covering the asphalt for twenty years, just looked me over, shook his head and stuck the Chevy into gear. He could tell I was from out of town.

Thirty minutes after I had arrived at the station for the second time, a long black diesel with a train of ribbed stainless steel eased in and discharged its stale passengers. Into the midst of elderly gentlemen adjusting their hats and porters hustling luggage stepped Elvis, his hair freshly slicked. He was draped in the same roomy suit I'd seen the day before and wearing that same sly smile. This time he was on his home turf and he knew it.

I said, "Hi, Elvis, how ya doin'. I made it."

He laughed. "Yeah, you sure did."

And he kept on walking, his cousin Junior in tow carrying the only piece of luggage. I was a little deflated, but by now I knew he wasn't one to make small talk and, after all, I was the one who wanted to be the unobtrusive fly on the wall.

As he passed through the sounds of the station — the diesel idling, trunks being slammed onto platforms, hard shoes hitting harder concrete — the music of spirituals moved with him. In his right hand was an RCA Victor "Transistor Seven" radio which looked like a briefcase with knobs on it. At the upper level, he changed stations and country and western music poured out. No one paid any mind.

As though he were another commuter, he picked up the *Richmond Times-Dispatch*, tucked it under his arm and sauntered past the main entrance and out the side exit through a bright, empty corridor. Elvis and his music flowed down that corridor with his hips swaying and his pants fluttering and his two-tones gliding. He was his own traveling show.

At the entrance to the Hotel Jefferson, a doorman dressed in an open-necked shirt met the cab. Junior took care of the fare, the neglected newspaper and the luggage, while Elvis took care of the radio. It wasn't until he had found some rock 'n' roll that we entered the hotel.

The Hotel Jefferson, "Showplace of the South," was a grand old building of indeterminate age, a Southern mixture of ancient Greece, Florentine Italy and King Arthur's Court. The lobby presented great high-backed chairs with wooden arms like rails, and immense marble columns that supported the mezzanine with carved mantels of fruit and rose another story to more fruit before they pushed through the ceiling. Below, a broad marble floor was bisected by a single strip of carpet from the door to the desk.

Into this sedate marble memorial strutted Mr. Presley and his rock 'n' roll. Two little old ladies perked up on one of King Arthur's couches and gave him the beady eye all the way to the desk. As Elvis leaned on the counter with his back to the mail slots, the clerk, recognizing him, stepped forward to sign him in, but before the clerk could say anything, Elvis abruptly turned his head and announced himself with a mock self-importance: "Elvis (dramatic pause) Presley." Then he presented that sly grin. I don't think the desk clerk understood it.

With his radio still reverberating rock 'n' roll, Elvis

stepped into the elevator. The operator didn't comment on the music, in fact, nobody in the hotel said a word. She just said, "Floor, please," and Junior said, "Four."

In the hotel's colonial restaurant, Elvis and Junior sat quietly without the radio. A breakfast of bacon, eggs over easy, milk, no coffee and home fries was capped off with a scoop of vanilla ice cream in cantaloupe. Eating is an experience people usually prefer to enjoy without the intrusion of a photographer, but Elvis didn't seem to care. As far as I could tell, nothing much seemed to bother him and if it did, he kept it to himself.

After breakfast we adjourned to the coffee shop across the lobby, Junior to the window with a cigar and Elvis to the magazine rack. It was stocked with *Look, Life, Colliers, The Saturday Evening Post* and the usual array of men's magazines, *Field and Stream, Cavalier, Man's Life.* He thumbed through the titles and chose a copy of *Quick,* about the size of *TV Guide* and with a cover that offered a brunette with a forty-inch superstructure and the question "Are Sex Dreams Normal?" An issue of *Man's World* told him "You could be SCARED TO DEATH." *Male Adventure* portrayed "Man against Snake" with a parade of cobras, pythons and rattlers, and then graduated to show some pictures of tame cheesecake. An old pensioner stepped up to study the pinups in *Cavalier.* Elvis moved on to *Screen* magazine with an article on Jerry Lewis, "A Mug for the Muggers."

After we killed about an hour, Elvis said he was going to his room to get some rest and he would see me later. That was fine by me; I was hungry and I needed an opportunity to collect my thoughts. I had to keep an eye on him because I never knew what he was going to do next. This would be the only chance to plot any strategy.

Over breakfast I caught up on the news from the *Richmond Times-Dispatch.* Polish workers were demonstrating in Poznan. Secretary of Defense Wilson disputed an "A-death" estimate, disclaiming any responsibility for the release of an army estimate that several hundred million deaths might result if the United States made a retaliatory nuclear attack on Russia. He thought the death estimate was "somewhat exaggerated." The Russians claimed they had "some very effective atomic weapons." They didn't give any details. The Su-

preme Court was asked to reject the NAACP bid on schools, Eisenhower signed a $33 billion road bill and Marilyn Monroe married Arthur Miller. On page 11, the Yankees whipped the Senators 3–1 and on page 21, surrounded by a herd of Western movie ads, Railey's Appliance Center presented Elvis Presley and his Stage Show at the Mosque Theatre at 5:00 and 8:00 P.M. Tickets were $2.50 and $2.00 for reserved seats, $1.50 for general admission. The box office would open at noon and plenty of good seats were available.

On a global scale, this might not seem particularly newsworthy, but for me it was the biggest news of the day. It was the first time I knew exactly where and when the show was going to take place.

I had expected to see the Colonel present in his capacity as supervisor. He wasn't at the hotel, neither were the musicians nor Elvis' guitar. I figured he probably was at the theater, and since Elvis was safely tucked away in his room, I decided to investigate.

The cab let me off at the corner of North Laurel and Main streets in ninety-two-degree heat. The streets were quiet. A black mother and her two daughters strolled under the shade of an umbrella and disappeared into the park across the street.

North Laurel and Main, two streets that could have been anywhere in the country, was a corner out of a sleepy little town in the "Twilight Zone," hot and silent and timeless. But I was not in the "Twilight Zone," and I was not in Richmond, I was in Jerusalem.

Next to a Gothic cathedral, which seemed to shrink in comparison, towered a massive brick building inscribed with Arabic signatures, vented with latticed windows and crowned with minarets. This mosque might have been taken for holy ground had it not been for the theater marquee. It read "Elvis Presley Sat. 5 and 8 P.M." I knew this must be the place.

It had more than a dozen doors, all locked tight. I checked my watch. It was past noon. The box office should have been open, but the Colonel was nowhere to be seen.

I found Elvis in the Jefferson coffee shop. His radio rested silently next to a bowl of chili. It was a coffee shop that any traveler would know: a row of red vinyl high chairs sat before a strip of formica and looked on an array of Campbell's soup cans, individual breakfast cereals and framed signs that proclaimed famous sandwiches (a grilled cheese could set you back twenty cents).

I was hot and sweaty and he was cool and clean, looking almost dignified in a slate-grey suit, pressed white shirt and white knit tie. It was the white bucks that gave him away.

A woman was with him. She wasn't interested in a quick lettuce and tomato. She was dressed for Saturday night. Her earrings were a dense constellation of rhinestones that framed a face full and mature beyond her years. (It seems all young women in those days looked older than their age.) Her short blond hair was sprayed in place, her eyebrows sharply penciled, her lips painted a soft red. She filled a basic black chemise held up by two thin straps and cradled a purse splashed with dime store pearls. Clear plastic high heels dangled from her feet.

She was trying to appear casual, not an easy task since a photographer was on the other side of the salt and pepper. Elvis was cool, "Oh, he's the photographer, that's okay, he's with me," as if to say it's only natural to have a photographer on a date. I'd have felt a little rigid, especially if I had turned and looked into the infinite eyes of his shadow, Junior, slouched on the far end of the counter, rotating a cigar with his fingertips.

I didn't know anything about her but it seemed as if Elvis was a sailor and this was one of his ports. She crossed her legs and in a soft Southern accent asked what he was reading. He was only too happy to oblige, telling her it was the script for the "Steve Allen Show" — "It's gonna be on tomorrow night, are you gonna see the show?" — and talking about learning his lines (he had a part in a skit) — "I'm Tumbleweed" — and saying that he was gonna be a cowboy with Steve Allen, Imogene Coca and Andy Griffith, and at the end, he was gonna pull his six-gun and shoot a candy bar. She seemed impressed.

Elvis set the script aside and finished his chili, and when he set that aside, he turned his full attention to her, talking about how nice her hair was and how pretty her earrings were. He was sweet and natural.

She smiled and properly thanked him. "Elvis, is it okay if I come backstage?"

"Sure, honey, shouldn't be any problem."

Then he grinned, leaned into her ear and said, "Maybe after the show . . ." and mumbled something for her ears only. He laughed, turned into my camera and mugged. A real joker.

Junior interrupted and told Elvis they had to go.

"Go where?" Elvis asked.

Junior wasn't in the mood. "C'mon, Elvis, we gotta go."

It was 4:30 P.M. and the show was going to start in half an hour. Elvis didn't seem too concerned. I guessed he had something else on his mind.

The cab drove up Main Street, drifting through the still heat until it landed at the rear of the Mosque Theatre. I had expected Elvis to march directly up the backstage ramp, — it was only twenty minutes to show time, — but, instead, he laid back and held court with the few young ladies who had gathered, all primly dressed in their Sunday best and ready with their Brownie cameras. For someone who was moving up pretty fast he never seemed to be in a rush. He always had time for the fans. The blonde in the black chemise and Junior stepped aside.

"Elvis, can my girlfriend take a picture of you and me?" asked one of the young ladies.

"Sure, honey."

"Elvis, are you going to sing "Heartbreak Hotel?"

"Maybe. Are you gonna watch me tomorrow night on television?"

"Oh, yes."

Elvis was not a celebrity who had some vague love of the people or a star who, with a wave of hands, would acknowledge some generalized gratitude for all who had made this possible. He was specific, giving his attention to each, as the Pope gives a personal audience. It was his fans who defined the word "devotion" and it was Elvis who was propagating the faith. He may not have known what he had but it was clear they knew he had it. I was still trying to find out what "it" was.

Backstage, musicians unpacked their instruments, reporters milled around looking for an opportunity, and young wives and mothers sat against the wall drinking Pepsi and smoking cigarettes. On stage, under the beam of spotlights, a small brass band rehearsed.

The stage was a shallow blond floor separated

from the audience by a thick fading red curtain. Through the curtain I could hear the theater filling up with conversation and the shouts of boys hawking programs.

Elvis wandered around the stage, feeling its size like a builder inspecting a piece of land. When he finished his survey he nodded to his musicians in the wings and proceeded toward what could be called the green room.

The green room in a theater is the traditional haven for performers, where they can take a moment, gather concentration and focus intent. Sometimes it is actually green. This particular room was neither green nor a haven. It was a small room with dusty beige walls, a clutter of creaky wooden chairs, coffee cups, empty Coke bottles, a clothes rack without hangers and a single window that overlooked the stage door ramp.

Two girls peeked through the window, watching Elvis, his musicians and the Jordanaires tuning up. They poked questions. "Elvis, are you going to sing 'Heartbreak Hotel'?" At first he ignored them, then he turned in an abrupt about-face and shot an "I see you" look. They screeched and ran, broadcasting "He looked at me, he looked at me." He laughed.

Elvis returned to his musicians. Scotty Moore, a lean young man who looked like he just got out of high school, picked his guitar with fast hands. D. J. Fontana tapped his drumsticks on a chair. D. J. had angular good looks, a Roman nose highlighted by a wide smile over a narrow chin, and hair swept back like fins on the sides of his head. Bill Black seemed destined to play the bass, his features were round and his body center-weighted. The Jordanaires — Gordon Stoker, Neal Matthews, Jr., Hoyt Hawkins and Hugh Jarrett — sang the background harmonies. They were one of the top vocal groups in country and western music, noted for their spirituals performed on the Grand Ole Opry.

Shrieks of "We love you, Elvis" came through the open window. The proper young ladies on the ramp had been displaced by a crowd of giggling junior-high-school girls loaded with photographs of Elvis. The shouting became obtrusive. Elvis stepped up to the window, triggering more screeches, until he said, "I can't talk now. I'll see you in the show later. Nice of you to come see me." That seemed to satisfy them for the moment. The rehearsal resumed and I left, wondering where the Colonel was.

The theater was filling up with dresses, hundreds of dresses: florals, pastels, some floating on layers of crinoline, some white-laced. There were few pants. Waves of Presley programs rolled back and forth, as people fanned themselves. There was no air conditioning and it was getting warm. A couple of the sheriff's deputies, dressed in blue, stood in the corners to make sure it didn't get too hot.

The lobby was jammed. More people were stacking up outside. Tom Diskin, the Colonel's right hand, was in the box office making change while the Colonel was hunched over in the middle of the crowd, breaking open bundles of souvenir programs and glossy photos suitable for framing. He gave a handful to a kid.

"Got enough change on ya, son? Make sure you count your change." The Colonel dispatched the kid and looked me over. "I see you got here, Wertheimer."

Everybody always seemed to be surprised when I showed up. I was too busy catching up to think about it.

The Colonel waved his cigar over his domain and announced, "Pretty impressive, eh?"

I hadn't seen this kind of a rush since opening day at Yankee Stadium. "Yeah, sure is, Colonel."

Then, as if he suddenly remembered the reason for all this, he asked, "How's Elvis doing?"

"I left him backstage rehearsing."

"Good, good. Well, I got work to do."

He went back to papering the lobby with glossies. Nowhere did I see any pictures of any other performers. It was wall-to-wall Elvis.

The green room was empty. I found Elvis chatting with some friends in the wings and since it was already past five, I decided this would be my only chance for a pit stop.

I am convinced there is a law of nature, as immutable as the rule of gravity, that dictates that whenever I am in the bathroom the phone will ring or the doorbell will sound. This time, the band started.

Just past the stage entrance is an iron staircase that leads to the bathroom upstairs and to the dressing rooms and the storage area downstairs. I scrambled down the steps, enraged that nature had forced me to miss Elvis's opening. Halfway down I came to an abrupt stop, for at the edge of the stairwell leading to the dressing rooms stood Elvis and the blonde in the black chemise.

He's supposed to be onstage and here he is fooling around, I thought. I couldn't figure it out. It didn't matter. He was here and so was I.

The afternoon light of a solitary window warmed the private corner and relieved the coldness of the harsh stucco and iron grillwork. The blonde leaned with her back against the wall, her hands holding her purse below her belt. Elvis had one hand resting on the railing and one foot on the first step leading down. They stood eye-to-eye.

I couldn't hear what they were saying, the music was reverberating in the stairwell, but the gestures were clear. Elvis was intent, and in that moment, she was the only one. But she wasn't easy. He was slow, natural, insistent. He slid his arms around her waist. She pressed her palms against his shoulders, pinning the purse between them. He inched forward. She retreated, grabbing the railing behind her to maintain her balance. He held her loosely behind her arched back, his eyelids sleepy, his lips pliant, and brushed a kiss against her cheek. Her soft smile made him bolder, and as her hands grasped the railing, he gently pulled her closer. She stuck her tongue out at him and he playfully returned the gesture. The tips of their tongues touched.

I was busy taking pictures, moving from the shadows into the light until I was so close I could touch them. Elvis knew I was there but couldn't have cared less. I eased by them for another shot. The documentarian in me said get the story, then my conscience said beat it. I left.

The act onstage was a square dance troupe. I learned later that this was one of Colonel Parker's routines: he'd hire acts out of various country and western circuits or variety shows and package them with Elvis when he toured the South. They got little or no billing. On this night the Colonel had hired Doris and Lee Strom, a dancing team; the Fliam Brothers, musical comedians; and Phil Maraquin, a magician.

The square dancers were given polite applause, and when the master of ceremonies came out to introduce the next act, he was greeted with a few calls of "Where's Elvis?"

Elvis was crouched in the wings watching the procession of acts. After the magician went through his tricks, the curtain closed, the applause fell away quickly and the shouts of "Where's Elvis?" became a chorus. The emcee asked the audience for their patience and assured them that Elvis was coming.

The comedians went into their routine while behind the curtain Scotty, D. J. and Bill set up their instruments. I took to the orchestra pit.

The crowd was restless and charged. The comedians were shuttled off with peremptory applause. The emcee moved quickly to center stage and introduced the Jordanaires. The curtain swung open and they contained the audience with a spiritual, which only compressed the anticipation.

The lights dimmed. A spotlight popped on, and Elvis rushed out onto the stage, propelled. There was an explosion, screaming, screeching, whistling, girls jumping, surging toward the stage.

Through it all came his voice, "Ah one for the money, Ah two for the show" and the show was on. He rolled the mike stand, rocked it, picked it up and carried it back and forth. He rippled, he shook. This was not the same Elvis I had seen on the Dorsey Brothers' "Stage Show." His body was not connected to the ground, he was moving too fast to touch it. Then he brought it all back down.

"Its always nice to be back in Richmond. This is something that, uh, we recorded a few weeks ago. I hope you like it."

"Ho-ho-hold me close, hold me tight ..." He was making love, he was down on his knees, and all the energy that had been bottled, that had been contained in those fervent breasts for what must have seemed forever, flared into a convulsive ecstasy that made me understand for the first time what a religious experience might be like. Whatever he had, he had a lot of it. Even I was high with excitement. The people at RCA, the executives who understood sales charts, trend lines and growth rates would say they didn't know why he was so popular. All they had to do was come down South and bear witness.

"I want you, I need you, I love you with all my heart." He was hot and wet; the girls were crying, smearing their faces with handkerchiefs, hugging each other, holding each other's hands, then reaching, grasping for him. Elvis kissed a hand, a forehead and before more fans could rush forth he moved back and cooled it off with a gospel song.

He sang to the first row, to the balcony, to the mothers and the grandmothers. He had an intuitive sense of the audience, for as soon as things started going out of control he'd back off. I had covered other entertainers before who had more experience, more learning in their craft but none felt an audience the way that Elvis did. Others had an act, Elvis had revelations. He had true emotion. He was so spontaneous, as I learned later, that the musicians often wouldn't know what he was going to sing next. He might give a cue or he might sing the first few words (as he did often in his recordings) and then the musicians would jump in.

The spotlight was on Elvis and behind him dim light formed the shapes of his musicians and the Jordanaires. By the time he finished the gospel song, the frenzy had boiled down to an applause, the grandmothers appreciating his voice and a few girls shouting names of songs they wanted to hear.

"Tomorrow night, I'm gonna be on the "Steve Allen Show." I hope y'all watch me. I hope I do well so you can be proud of me." Then he growled. "Let's get real gone." And bang, "Ah wop baba loo ah boo lop bam boom . . ."

The burners were all the way up. Just when he had them cooled down he put the flame to them. He fluttered, he sprang, he gave you a feeling of tremendous speed. I was tuned on Mozart and the Big Bands and didn't feel particularly susceptible to pop fads, but this was overpowering. It was not a matter of one's taste in music, it was a question of whether or not you considered yourself a living, animate human being. Elvis on a record or on TV might be different, remote, otherworldly, but live, he was powerful, penetrating, shattering, exhausting. Parents weren't afraid of his so-called bump and grind, they were afraid of his power.

Elvis changed up again. He burned bright, then he burned blue, then he burned deep in the third degree. The curtain swung closed, the band continued and Elvis dodged into the wings. Two thousand girls screamed, "More, more, please, please come back, Elvis!" The curtain parted and their lover strutted back before outstretched arms and red puffy faces. Before the mike, he caught his breath and with his voice coming from deep down, he said,

"I have to save some of myself for the next performance, but you've been such a good audience, that, uh, I'd like to sing this for you."

He pulled the mike to his mouth, gathered as much air as his lungs could hold, leaned back and let the last row know, "Waahl, since my baby left me, I found a new place to dwell . . ."

That ripped it. There was still screaming but not

with the same release that had met his opening. They had crossed over into the region of the possessed and the saved. The hold now was too powerful to be released by crying or screaming, there was nothing to do except to surrender. With the light from the stage, I could look into the first ten rows and see girls just standing there, their eyes fixed on somewhere between Elvis and eternity.

Elvis waved good-bye, the musicians played exit music behind the closing curtain and the house lights went up. The emcee's announcement of the next show was buried under cries of "We want Elvis!"

The Colonel was right. It was impressive. All of this had taken place in less than half an hour. And, no doubt, he knew what it was worth.

Elvis came into the wings exhausted, with his white shirt soaked, his hair disheveled, his eyes glazed. Instead of retreating to a private space, like other performers with whom I had worked, Elvis took a seat outside the green room in the middle of all the activity going on backstage. The blonde in the black chemise, his cousin Junior and a little blond girl stood at his side and watched him silently comb his hair. The drain of the performance didn't add the age that fatigue brings; Elvis looked younger, like a kid just out of high school.

Somebody gave him a Pepsi, and as soon as he joined the present, the momentum of his nervous energy sent him back to center stage where he sat down and started playing with the drums. A reporter in bow tie and glasses pulled up a chair and asked questions like he was covering a fire and Elvis was the fire chief. He wanted the facts. It was a refreshing change from New York reporters asking why he was lewd.

"Elvis, where did you learn to sing?"

"Well, I've been singing ever since I can remember. I didn't learn it, I mean, nobody taught it to me."

"Do you write your own songs?"

"No, I don't write my own songs. People send in demos. I choose my own songs."

"Do you make your own arrangements?"

"Not exactly, uh, I listen to the demos and, uh, you know, we work it out."

"Are you going to try anything with a full orchestra?"

"Not yet, haven't gotten around to trying that yet."

As the reporter filled in the answers to his prepared questions, Elvis fiddled with the drumsticks, tapping them on his hands, setting them down, then picking them up and bumping them against his chin. The little blond girl sat at his side and played with her own drumstick. Elvis always seemed to have a playmate. The reporter asked,

"Are the Jordanaires part of your regular back-up group?"

"Yes, sir, we just started working together recently."

"When are you going to do your first movie?"

"I've done a screen test for Hal Wallis, but nothin' has been signed, maybe something will come of it by the end of the year, but you'd have to talk to the Colonel, the Colonel would know more about that."

The reporter scratched down the news. Before he had a chance to hear another question, Elvis was on his way to the piano in the orchestra pit, his playmate right behind. He tossed the white cover aside, pulled over a couple of chairs — "Here, honey, you sit here" — and together they banged out "Chopsticks," Elvis attacking the pedals with his white bucks. At the end of this duet, Elvis turned to a few fans leaning over the railing and deadpanned, "See, anybody can be a musician." The girls at the railing giggled. The reporter still had his fire to cover.

"Elvis, are you going with anybody steady right now?"

He slid to the edge of his seat, letting an arm dangle over its back and resting a leg on an empty chair. It was the first time since the end of the first show that Elvis assumed a position anyone might call relaxed.

"Well, when the right one comes along, maybe I'll settle down, but right now I haven't found the right one." It was an answer the girls at the rail approved.

"What kind of girls do you like — blond, red-head or brunette?"

"I like all girls. I like 'em all."

"Do you have a fence around your house?"

"No, sir, we just have a big front lawn."

"Do people bother you, do you get bothered a lot when people come barging through your house or onto your lawn?"

"It's not nice when they trample down the grass,

but I don't mind people coming up into the driveway. Sometimes, Ma will invite them in to have some sandwiches or sit around the pool."

As the reporter filled his notebook, Elvis wandered into the wings looking for something to do. He found an outlet in the green room. It wasn't the blonde in the black chemise, it was an accordion.

He strapped it on and played it as if it were his own. The reporter persisted. Elvis wasn't evading him, he just had to have something to play with. While Elvis squeezed out a tune, the reporter squeezed in his questions.

"Elvis, are you going on a road tour?"

"Yes, sir."

"What cities are you going to see?"

"I don't know them all exactly, the Colonel would know more about that."

"How do you feel working on the road?"

"Tired."

"How do you feel about the press, do you feel that they're unfair to you?"

"Well, they got a job to do and I'm doing what I feel is right. I can't tell them what to write about me, I can just go ahead and do what I think is right."

The audience for the second show was slightly older than the first but no less demanding. They were old enough for serious dating, but from what I could see in the theater, their date that night was Elvis.

He stepped out wearing a bright green jacket, which, against the red curtain, made him glow like a traffic light. Elvis did what he thought was right and it was. He knew when to change gears, when to speed to the edge of the cliff, when to pull over and turn out the lights. If they had spent an hour and a half getting ready, setting their hair, making up, wondering what earrings to wear, it didn't matter now; there was no rule of decorum (it was too hot to be genteel), there was only that last desperate grasp to keep from being so totally released that there was no hope of returning. They had to scream.

"Shake, rattle and roll"

"You won't do right to save your natural soul . . ."

And when they had peaked, Elvis, out of breath and spent, smiled and said "Thank you." Then he walked out.

The master of ceremonies took a tenuous hold of center stage. The musicians behind him charged through an Elvis medley while the crowd up front made Yankee Stadium sound minor league. "We want Elvis," "We love you, Elvis," "Where's Elvis?"

The emcee offered, "We'll try and get Elvis back."

The curtain swung tight and the band's medley burst to the finish. Over the crescendo of applause and screaming, the emcee shouted the farewell, "You've been a great audience and we appreciate the warm welcome we've had here in Richmond tonight. Elvis appreciates it and all our other wonderful entertainers appreciate it. Thank you."

The house lights went up. Just when it looked like it was all over, that there was no hope for their lover's return, the curtain opened again and the band started another medley. Everyone was confused. As if that one brief moment of indecision was a challenge to their faith, they rushed, some to the stage, some to the exits, leaving the fainthearted applauding numbly in the aisles and those with broken hearts crying in their seats. I climbed backstage as the musicians brought down the final curtain, expecting to find Elvis hiding in the green room behind the protection of the local deputies. Before I reached the wings, I realized Elvis was not in the theater. He had already escaped.

A bare bulb over the stage door lit a swarm of fans that surrounded Elvis' musicians and members of the other acts as they dodged their way out. One of the relentless asked Scotty, "Is Elvis still in the building?" He claimed that he didn't think so but he couldn't be sure. Nobody believed him. Someone shouted that Elvis was coming out from the other side of the theater. A squad raced around the corner before another girl down the ramp shouted, "No, he's not, he came out this exit ten minutes ago and left."

A teary-eyed girl wailed, "That's not true."

"It is so."

Behind me, a teenager asked her friend, "Are you sure he left?"

"Yes, he went in the sheriff's car."

"Where did he go?"

"I don't know."

"Are you *sure* he left?"

"Look, I got his autograph."

Hard evidence. The teenager's disbelief that her idol had beat it out the back door turned into a frustration directed squarely at the musicians.

"That's not fair, we waited all day. We came all the way from Stony Creek. We wanted to see Elvis. I was hoping to talk to Elvis and touch him, now he's gone, and I don't think that's fair." She didn't bother to ask for Scotty's autograph.

The crowd dispersed, leaving a few of the truly devoted. A zealot asked Bill, who was relaxing a moment, smoking a cigarette on the edge of the ramp, "Where are you going?" Bill flicked an ash and looked into the parking lot where the other entertainers were packing up. "We're going to eat somewhere on the road. We're going to go to a restaurant." He was pretty convincing. I had no idea where we were going. I whispered, "How are you getting back to New York?" He looked at his watch. "Well, we gotta get to the train station and catch the 10:50." I thought, great, that gives me twenty minutes to get there and the streets are jammed with traffic.

"How do I get there?"

"Follow me."

Under the marquee at the front of the theater was a sheriff's paddy wagon. Some girls were still running around the theater with their autograph books and souvenir programs, while a few stood hopelessly stranded on the sidewalk. A deputy held open a door at the rear of the black and white paddy wagon. Bill told me to hop in, that it was the only way out.

The inside of the wagon was dark. Through the wire mesh windows I could see people wandering around, but that view dissolved into a succession of streetlights. A quiet conversation in front softened the scratch of the police radio. The darkness was a relief, like sleeping with your eyes open, only the dreams didn't come to unravel it all and make the connections so you could forget it all and go on. I was watching a movie, I was in a movie, moving, gone, gonna get real gone, didn't he say gone, yeah, get real, real gone. I was.

The door clicked open. We were at the train station, five minutes till departure. We ran down the halls, down the stairs, into the Pullman. Where's Elvis? In the sleeper. He was in the upper berth, his hand on his forehead, his eyes on the ceiling, watching his own movie.

With his date for the day and his two cousins, Carroll "Junior," top, and Gene Smith, bottom. Hotel Jefferson coffee shop, Richmond, June 30, 1956.

En route in a cab to the Mosque Theatre, with his date and "Junior." Elvis has her in the palm of his hand.

(Next page) Instead of entering the Mosque Theatre immediately upon arrival, Elvis poses with his fans for a few pictures. To the right of Elvis in the white jacket is D. J. Fontana, his drummer.

(Preceding page)
Fans on the stage-
door ramp of the
Mosque Theatre
listen to the
sounds coming
through an
open window
of Elvis and the
Jordanaires
warming up.

With the Jordan-
aires in the men's
lavatory, which
had to serve as
their dressing
room.

During rehearsal,
Elvis tries to hear
the Jordanaires
over the scream-
ing of his fans
outside.

Elvis entertains his date, while other performers are doing their acts on stage.

(Following page) Sticking her tongue out at him doesn't check his advance, it only makes him bolder.

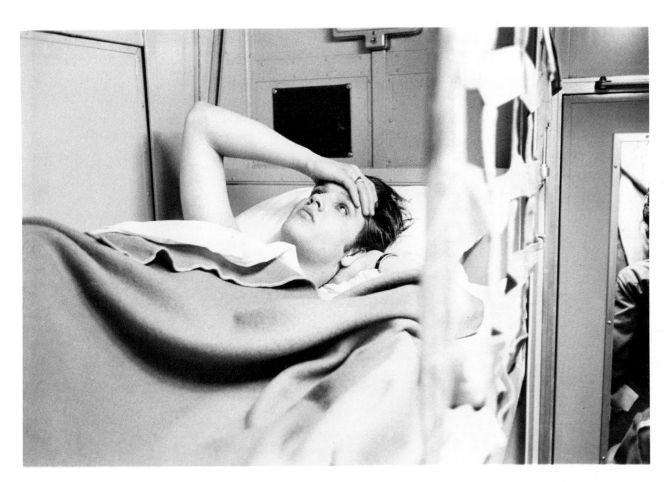

On the train back
to New York and
the "Steve Allen
Show," exhausted
after two perfor-
mances and a
quick exit.

Blue Tie & Tails

"It's not too often that I get to wear the, uh ... suit an' tails."

I woke up in Newark, New Jersey, feeling sticky. We were fifteen minutes from New York, and with a cold shot of water on the face and my all-American breakfast of an apple, a half-pint of milk and a Yankee Doodle cupcake, I was ready to go.

Elvis was sitting cross-legged in a compartment with D. J. and Bill. He had on the same white bucks as the night before, which were no longer quite so white, the same slate-grey suit and the same slick pompadour, which by now had a gloss that could outshine a waxed black Cadillac.

He was reading a fan letter. D.J. studied her photograph, a wallet-sized high school picture that was so universal in kind, I was convinced there was a special camera that, no matter how it was used, would forever yield a "cheese" smile looking over the right shoulder. D.J. turned it over to read her name and handed it to Elvis, whose face was still puffy and soft from sleep. Elvis looked her over and passed into a morning daydream.

D. J. said, "Hey, she's pretty good lookin', huh?"
Elvis came back. "Yeah, pretty good lookin'."

Bill looked out the window and all went black. We were crossing under the Hudson River into the subterranean corridors of Pennsylvania Station.

The main concourse of the station was active with Sunday morning travelers. Elvis picked up a copy of the Sunday *New York Mirror*. This time he didn't stick it under his arm. In bold, two-inch type the headline read "2 Airliners Missing, 127 Aboard." I had heard he once had a close call in a chartered plane, somewhere outside of Texas.

He read that news across the concourse "PHOENIX, ARIZ. June 30. Two luxury airliners, carrying an estimated 127 passengers and crew,

were missing and presumed crashed in the Arizona desert ..."), up the stairs ("as darkness wrapped the desert, a vast search-rescue effort was halted for the night ..."), on the street ("... could be the worst disaster in commercial aviation history ...") and in the cab ("Other Major Flying Disasters") to the Hudson Theatre, site of the "Steve Allen Show." The train looked better all the time.

If he had turned to the television section on page 48, he would have discovered this little tidbit by columnist Nick Kenny.

Will Elvis rock and wriggle on Steve Allen's Show tonight??? While thirty million teenage fans applaud in wild delight??? And will he shake his torso like a trotter with the heaves??? While pear-shaped notes of purest gold tell how his poor heart grieves??? Will Presley's fans all rally at the nearest TV set??? While mom and pop retire just as far as they can get??? Will maidens swoon and lads grow faint when Elvis starts to squeal??? And who can Sullivan dig up to fight such (ugh) appeal???

This is the question of the hour ... in just so many words .... Is good taste just a mockery??? Is talent for the birds??? Some guys don't care what they air when ratings are too lean .... But I'm convinced that Presley should be heard and never seen!!!

Somewhere the sun is shining bright and there is peace somewhere .... Somewhere there's not a cloud in sight — no Elvis in the air .... Somewhere there are no TV sets and I wish that I were there!!!

We were back in New York. The number four Mirror Disc of the Week was "I Want You, I Need You, I Love You" by Sivle Yelserp (*sic*). Number one was "Wayward Wind" by Gogi Grant. The frosting on the cake was one of "Nick's Snacks!!!": "It isn't what young girls know that bothers their parents ... it's how they found out."

The cab carrying Tom Diskin, Elvis, Junior and myself drove up Forty-fourth Street, which was deserted and grey under the Sunday morning overcast. At the entrance to the theater, a young girl dressed all in white appeared, escorted by a middle-aged gentleman. She looked about sixteen going on thirty, and wore what must have been her best white dress (its billowing folds were topped by a bow in the back), white gloves, white pumps, and white hat. Her earrings were white rhinestones in the shape of hearts. Around her neck was a rhinestone cross. She looked as if she were ready for her first Communion, except for the dark glasses that she wore.

As soon as Elvis opened the door of the cab, she bravely stepped forward and with all the tentative confidence mental rehearsals bring, she asked, "Elvis, can I have your autograph?"

"Sure, honey."

She presented the pen and the book. He asked her name and she told him, becoming so excited that she could barely speak. When it finally came out, it rushed in a choking torrent.

"I came in all the way from Long Island with my father; we've been waiting here for over an hour; I'm so lucky I was able to see you before you went into the theater; I can't wait to see you tonight."

Elvis returned her autograph book, took a white-gloved hand in both of his and smiled graciously.

"It's very nice of you to come all the way from Long Island. I really appreciate it."

She choked again. "I'm, I'm so happy to see you. I love your music. I love your voice; I've got all your records; I love "I Want You, I Need You, I Love You"; I listen to it all the time; I read everything I can about you. . . ."

She couldn't go on.

Elvis spoke gently. "I'm glad you like it. I sure hope I do well tonight. You gonna watch?"

"I sure will."

Tom interrupted. "Elvis, it's getting to be time for rehearsal."

"I gotta go now."

She kept it together. "Goodbye."

As soon as Elvis entered the theater, she covered her face and wept. Her father put his arm around her, delighted that his daughter's wish had come true. I asked to take their picture. She composed herself for one shot, then covered her face again and burst into tears. It was true devotion. After the scene last night, I believed it.

In the dressing room, Elvis washed his face and combed his hair. A balding man dressed in shirt-sleeves and tie appeared in the open doorway. "Mr. Presley?"

"You can call me Elvis."

"Okay, Elvis, Mr. Allen would like to see every-body in the orchestra area in about ten minutes."

"I'll be there."

The man closed the door as he left. Elvis took a good look in the mirror and combed his hair just right.

The Hudson Theatre, the oldest legitimate showhouse on Broadway, a relic of green marble and stained glass, had been overtaken by the unforgiving progress of television and had been converted into a studio. The stage, which had been extended to accommodate both sets and television cameras, jutted deep into the seating area leaving no more than a dozen rows. The balcony had been given over to the lights.

Elvis met Bill and D. J. outside his dressing room and they quietly walked together across the stage and up the aisle and took seats halfway from the rear where Tom and a few of the Jordanaires sat. The Colonel was nowhere in sight.

Scattered around them were the people that made a live television show; they were also an audience. Elvis was no longer home, he was in New York. He was surrounded by professionals and established stars and if they had any doubts about him, he had to be convincing when he got his chance.

Steve Allen was seated in a Victorian living room set talking to the director about an article he was reading in the Sunday *New York Times*. After everyone was assembled, Steve took to the aisle, and as he paced back and forth, detailed the outline of the show with a lighthearted humor that was itself an act. He listed the order of the acts and mentioned appearances by Eydie Gorme, Steve Lawrence and Milton Berle, in addition to Andy Griffith, Imogene Coca, and Elvis.

Talent was stacking up like trophies on a mantel. Ten blocks and a couple of Trendex points away, Ed Sullivan would mount his campaign with a newspaper ad announcing the appearances of: "John Huston, Jose Ferrer, Orson Welles, Edward G. Robinson, Lauren Bacall, Vincent Price, Billy Pearson, Burl Ives — and many others — and Gregory Peck re-enacting scenes from the mighty new Warner Bros. production of "Moby Dick." In an era that allowed few alternatives, this was, at least, a real choice: Captain Ahab or the Memphis Flash.

Steve finished his outline and after a ten-minute break, the first run-through began. Stagehands shuttled props, sound booms descended and Imogene and Steve played husband and wife. A voice heard over the public-address system instructed the actors in their positions as stagehands taped the floor with different camera coordinates.

The public-address called Elvis to the stage. The musicians and the Jordanaires walked onto a set that could have been designed by Aristotle and Liberace. In the background, Greek columns in perspective pointed to an urn of overflowing vines. On the sides, plaster nymphs cradled candelabra and overhead, chandeliers provided the final offering to the classics of western civilization. At the foot of this temple stood Elvis.

The voice over the PA announced, "Okay Elvis, anytime you're ready." With his arms hanging as loose by his side as the guitar hanging around his neck, Elvis counted the beat with his leg and crooned "I Want You, I Need You, I Love You." He sang without the passion I had seen in Richmond. He sang like a professional who had his act down pat. He was competent. He didn't move, he didn't touch the microphone, he stood square, both feet spread and stuck to the ground.

After he had finished, the audience of professionals applauded. Steve patted him on the back and told him it was great. Elvis smiled and in a slow, modest voice, he said, "Thank you, Mr. Allen."

A stagehand shoved a platform to the microphone and was followed by a trainer with a female basset hound. As he dressed her in collar, bow tie and top hat, Elvis laughed and the audience laughed with him. The dog's woeful eyes seemed even more disconsolate with the constraints of her formal attire.

Elvis was instructed to sing to the dog. Without the mike, he crouched down nose-to-nose with the dog and let her know, "you ain't nothing but a hound dog." She heard that and ignored him for the rest of the song.

Now they had a problem. Steve wanted the hound to listen to Elvis, so he suggested that they get to know each other. The top hat and bow tie were removed. Elvis leaned over, caressed her neck and whispered in her ear. She turned away. Elvis became intimate, speaking softly, touching her forehead with his hand to let her know she was the only one in his life. She didn't believe him.

The director tried his technique, scratching her chin and speaking his own special dog language. He convinced her to put aside her feelings and be the trooper he knew she was.

The director gave the cue. Elvis extended his hand and she leaned forward and rested her chin in his palm. He told her again she was nothing but a hound dog, and when he had her where he wanted her, his hand holding her face close to his, he told her she "ain't never caught a rabbit." Elvis tried to keep a straight face when she turned away. Scotty, D. J. and Bill rocked through the refrain.

Elvis coiled like a runner at the starting blocks, shot his finger straight out at her and told her again. She looked right back at him and took it, and when he finished telling her, "you ain't no friend of mine," he patched it all up, hugging and caressing her, laughing as she licked his face. The audience applauded, the stagehands nodded, and Steve approved. The Memphis Flash was okay.

Even with a positive reception from the assembly of journeymen, his slow Southern style of speaking — halting at times — made him appear unsure of himself. He was working with established stars and still remained a little in awe of them, never addressing them by their first names. The sketch they were to perform would be Elvis's first opportunity to act on live television, and though his part was small, it was still a part that he would have to portray with the same ease and spontaneity as his veteran partners had exhibited.

The rehearsal of the skit began immediately after the hound dog act. Steve, Andy and Imogene kept it lighthearted and easygoing, and with their support, Elvis relaxed into the natural fellow I had come to know.

The rehearsal went smoothly; most of the energy was directed to blocking the actors' movements and coordinating the cameras. Steve did most of the talking and when it came to Elvis, he was on cue and at home.

The dressing room was filled with reporters waiting for their target. The "Steve Allen Show" was Elvis' first appearance in New York since the Dorsey Brothers "Stage Show" three months earlier and, in that short time, his "gyrations" had already provoked a heated press. The major news syndicates were based in New York, so Elvis would have to give their people more attention than he had given the reporter in Richmond.

Elvis relaxed in a chair in the back corner of the cramped dressing room, crossing his legs before a legion that stood shoulder-to-shoulder. At his side appeared the Colonel and his lieutenant, Tom Diskin.

At the beginning of the conference, the reporters poked and probed for a chink in the defensive armor which they had assumed would be present.

"What do you think about the criticism you've been getting? Do you get mad when they call you Elvis the Pelvis?"

"Well, I think that's a pretty dumb comment. I can't tell reporters what to say, you know, they have a job that they have to do and I can just do what I think is right."

"Are you nervous about your performance tonight in front of a national audience?"

"No, sir, I think I'm prepared."

"What do you think about the skit?"

"It's pretty funny."

"Have you ever worked with Imogene Coca and Andy Griffith before?"

"No, sir, but I'm looking forward to it. They're some of my favorite performers."

Elvis answered simply and directly. His accent flowed with the nonchalance of front porch conversation and the charm of a Southern gentleman. The press came looking for a hillbilly yokel. He gave them amazing grace. I was impressed. So were the reporters.

When they realized they were not dealing with a naive out-of-towner, they retreated and lapsed into the usual overworked angles about his personal life. Is he going with anyone steady? What kind of girls did he like? What's his favorite food? And so forth. No one asked about his music. Here I was in New York, the newspaper town with nearly a dozen major dailies, and not one reporter asked about his music. They were so preoccupied with digging for sensational tidbits that they missed what I thought was the real story: Elvis and his music made the girls cry.

The Colonel interceded, allowed a few more questions and mentioned that he had to talk to Elvis. That was the end of the conference. Before the reporters left they asked for his autograph, the women for themselves, the men for their wives.

I had been on the move since Friday night and the break time I had before the dress rehearsal would be my only opportunity to eat, change clothes and replenish my film supply.

When I returned to the theater, Anne Fulchino met me backstage with a story. After rehearsal Elvis had disappeared, neglecting to tell anyone where he was going. Acting on a hunch, Anne found him in a penny arcade on Broadway a few blocks away. Unhappy that he had been instructed not to move when he sang, Elvis had decided to blow off some steam playing pinball.

By the time I reached his dressing room, Elvis had resigned himself to his fate — a starched baby blue shirt, matching bow tie, tails and blue suede shoes. The elegance of his formal attire might have qualified him for an ambassador's ball, but his slicked hair and leering smile made him look like a party crasher.

While the other performers went through their paces in the dress rehearsal, Elvis stood calmly in the wings, hands in his pockets, waiting for his cue. Milton Berle walked over. He straightened Elvis' bow tie, grabbed his shoulder and told him like an uncle, "Good luck, kid." It was Elvis' two appearances on Berle's show that had scandalized the press. Elvis grinned and replied with his Southern charm, "Thank ya, Mr. Berle."

After the dress rehearsal, I climbed to a second-story walkway for a bird's-eye view of the stage and noticed the Colonel, without the straw hat he wore to cover his thinning hair, getting chummy with two show businessmen. Berle wandered by wearing a set of false sideburns, his joke for the show. When the Colonel saw me and his opportunity, he steered Berle around. Andy Griffith was on his way to the stage when the Colonel collared him, too. With his long arms gathering the two businessmen, Berle, and Griffith by the shoulders like Daddy Bear and his cubs, he looked up and shouted, "Wertheimer, take the picture." It was the kind of photograph that would end up suitably framed in the Colonel's office in Tennessee to let everyone know the Colonel was major league.

On July first, at eight o'clock eastern daylight time NBC presented the second national "Steve Allen Show," with Skitch Henderson and his twenty-nine piece orchestra and announcer Gene Rayburn.

Elvis and the stagehands watched the monitor in the wings. Steve played the piano, Uncle Milty got a plaque, Swami Steve walked on burning coals, Coca played wife to Allen's husband, Steve Lawrence and Eydie Gorme sang and Andy did an Arkansas version of Hamlet. The curtain closed. Steve took center stage, speaking in the rapid-fire there-are-not-enough-hours-in-a-twenty-four-hour-day clip of a New Yorker.

"Well, you know, a couple of weeks ago on the "Milton Berle Show," our next guest, Elvis Presley, received a great deal of attention which some people seemed to interpret one way and some viewers interpreted another. Naturally, it's our intention to do nothing but a good show.

Behind the curtain the hound yelped.

"Somebody is barking back there. We want to do a show the whole family can watch and enjoy and we always do and, tonight, we're presenting Elvis Presley in his — heh, heh — what you might call his first comeback . . ."

Steve and the audience chuckled.

". . . and at this time, it gives me extreme pleasure to introduce the new Elvis Presley. Here he is."

Amid the sounds of the orchestra's serenade and the audience's enthusiastic but polite applause, Elvis rambled into the lights and faced the camera in his tailored set of tails. He held his guitar by the neck, letting it stand at his side. Steve sped on.

"Elvis, I must say you look absolutely wonderful, you really do, and I think your millions of fans are really going to get kind of a kick seeing a different side of your personality tonight."

"Well, uh . . ." Elvis paused, lost in the long and painful moment of an actor trying to find his place. Allen's quick delivery made Elvis' Southern style seem so slow that his timing barely moved at all.

"Thank you, Mr. Allen . . . uh . . ."

Steve jumped in to help. "Can I hold your guitar here?"

Elvis found his place. "It's not too often that I get to wear the, uh . . . suit an' tails . . ." Steve prodded with an "uh-huh" as Elvis swallowed, ". . . and all this stuff."

The Elvis beat stepped up to New York time. "But, uh, I think I have on something tonight that's not quite correct for evening wear."

"Not quite formal? What's that, Elvis?"

"Blue suede shoes."

The audience laughed and applauded, cued less by Elvis' deadpan punchline than by Steve's wailing in mock surprise, "Oooh, yes." Steve got on with the show.

"Well, Elvis, you're certainly being a real good sport about the whole thing and now I have a little surprise for you. Gene, could I have the surprise?"

Gene handed him a huge roll of paper. "There you are."

"Thank you, Gene Rayburn. This, Elvis, believe it or not, is a giant petition that was signed by three giants out in the alley." The audience guffawed.

"No, seriously, this was signed by over eighteen thousand of Elvis' loyal fans saying we wanted to see him again soon on television. It was sent in to us just the other day by our good friend D. J. "Don" Wallace in Tulsa, Oklahoma. Eighteen thousand signatures on this. Elvis, it's a fine thing . . ." Applause finished the line.

In a low, reticent voice, Elvis replied, "It's wonderful, Mr. Allen. I'd like to thank — I'd like to thank all those — all those wonderful folks and I'd like to thank you, too."

"Well, that's okay, Elvis. Now watcha gonna — say what are you going to sing first for us tonight?"

" 'I Want You, I Need You, I Love You.' " Above the sounds of a generous ovation and some squelched screams, Steve cheered, "Here is the big RCA hit, Elvis."

Elvis put on his guitar as the curtain opened to reveal his musicians stationed in the temple. The Jordanaires waited at a mike offstage. Elvis looked at the monitor in the opposite wing and with his right hand at his side, set the time. Scotty plucked the line and as the second measure came over, Elvis pulled the mike toward himself, leaned back and exhaled his loving plea. "Ho-ho-hold me close, hold me tight."

The audience listened quietly. Elvis stayed in control, rocking gently. It was true. His body was an instrument, as essential to his sound as Scotty's country strains or Bill's blue bass. Putting Elvis in a suit and tails was like putting the great classical pianist, Artur Rubinstein, in rubber gloves. He couldn't release himself, he couldn't make you cry. But you still couldn't forget the voice.

When he finished, the audience cheered. Someone let out a "whoopee." Allen breezed onstage, and with the speed of a contestant on "Beat The Clock," said it was wonderful, predicted his new record "Hound Dog" was going to be a hit, presented the basset hound, took Elvis' guitar and, with an "away you go," made his exit.

Elvis never got a word out, he just looked at the dog and smiled with resignation. The hound, strapped in her top hat and collar, stood rigidly on the platform, facing the audience with an expression of profound boredom, like some dull stone statue ensconced at the foot of the Museum of Natural History with the inscription "Modern Dog." The audience giggled.

Without any further introduction, Elvis grabbed the mike and let her have it. As he had been instructed, he focused his attention on the hound. She didn't budge. He crouched, he circled, he paced back and forth, and though he didn't dance, he was still moving enough to draw a few squeals from the audience.

When he told her again she "ain't nothin' but a hound dog," he laughed and almost broke time, and after he told her "you ain't no friend of mine," he kissed her and strutted off the stage to cheering applause.

The takeoff on the Grand Ole Opry began with "Turkey in the Straw" and a lot of barnyard hooting and hollering. The set was a Broadway version of the interior of a barn; beams and windows painted on canvas flats, neatly arranged bales of hay, wagon wheels and wooden barrels. Everyone looked like dime store cowboys, with Elvis outfitted in a black shirt, red bandanna, black cowboy hat and a studded black leather holster with a six-shooter.

"Your old pardner, Big Steve" rambled on about how good it was to be out in the Old West, watching corrals on the trail, longhorning coyotes, and hogtying sagebrush, and more malapropisms from the old range, ending each speech with a "Right, gang?" Andy, Imogene and Elvis all hooted that it was.

The introductions of the gang ran on with more cornball from the prairie, with Big Steve giving Elvis this opener.

"I'll tell about this fella. He is a trick rider. You ain't seen trick riding until you've seen Tumbleweed: Yesterday, he went across the range on a full gallop blindfolded and he picked up a rattlesnake with his teeth; he jumped four fences and he dropped that snake into a gopher hole at a full gallop. Tell 'em why it was so tough, Tumbleweed?"

Elvis deadpanned. "I don't use no horse."

He got a laugh. Steve tore into a satire of a candy bar commercial, with everyone chiming in their bit. Elvis got the tag line.

"Don't forget, friends, that the Tonto Bar is made by the Kemo Sabe Candy Company in Ptomaine, Texas."

When Steve opened the candy bar, it jumped out of his hands like a live mouse, prompting great screaming and yelling, until Elvis shot it dead with his six-gun.

The skit closed with a parody of a country and western song, full of "yippy aye oh ky ayes," with each performer delivering a verse. When it was finally Elvis' turn, he strummed his guitar and sang in a voice as flat as the music,

Well, I gotta horse
And I gotta gun
And I'm going out and have some fun
I'm awarnin' you galoots
Don't step on my blue suede boots.

Skitch·ended it with a blast from the horn section and the audience received the performance with dutiful applause.

After the show, Allen congratulated Elvis on a job well done, Milton congratulated Steve and the stagehands congratulated each other. Elvis remained on stage to sign autographs for the few moon-eyed daughters who had gathered at the first row. With the houselights on, I had my first opportunity to see who was present. The assembly looked mature; it seemed there had been a selective admission.

On his way to the dressing room, Elvis was intercepted by the William Morris agent with the wire-rimmed glasses whom I had seen Friday morning at the first rehearsal. Shaking Elvis' hand, he said, "I think the show was terrific. You did a marvelous job. We really ought to get a good reaction to this one."

Tom Diskin, the Colonel's lieutenant, stood by with a wide smile.

The following morning in the *New York Journal-American*, Jack O'Brien's column was headlined in twenty-four point type: "Presley Gets the 'Brakes.' "

Elvis Presley was a cowed kid on Steve Allen's
opus last night. . . . NBC's promise to de-gyrate
the controversial hip-swingin' singer was kept. . . .
It proved Presley's excitement is not his voice but
his erotic presentation . . . . Best "guests" on the
show were Eydie Gorme and Steve Lawrence. . . .

As for the Pelvis, once his gears were shifted into a picture suitable for a Sunday evening, it was plain he couldn't sing or act a lick . . . .

In the *New York Times*, Jack Gould concurred.

Elvis Presley was a most sedate individual last night . . . his distasteful gyrations were eliminated . . . . Insofar as this corner is concerned the young man has lost none of his indescribable monotony as a singer . . . . If Mr. Presley behaves himself in other respects, he now is certainly entitled to pursue his career on TV.

Nick Kenny of the *New York Mirror* noted in his opening line,

Steve Allen topped Ed Sullivan by 20.2 to 14.8 in the Trendex rating . . . .

Back in his roomy suit and white bucks, Elvis relaxed in his dressing room combing his hair, happy that it was all over. The tails were piled in a heap on a chair.

A blue wedge of New York's finest escorted him through the theater and out the front door, taking the milling crowd by surprise. The fans were older and less passionate than those in Richmond, but no less devoted. Elvis climbed onto the trunk of a white Buick convertible and was promptly given requests for autographs. Some of the officers themselves handed slips of paper for the fans, but Elvis could manage to write only a few before the Buick eased him away into the night.

Inside, the theater was dim and cavernous. The sets onstage had been replaced by an empty ladder. A few stagehands chatted by the ropes. It seemed as if nothing had happened. I picked up my gear and walked out.

At the backstage exit, I heard girls giggling. Pushing against the wrought-iron gates of the Hudson Theatre was the throng of young teenagers I had missed out front. As I took their picture, they got all excited from the flashgun. Where there's a photographer, there must be a celebrity.

"Is Elvis coming out soon?" they asked.

I broke the bad news. "Elvis already went out through the front entrance."

They stopped giggling. "How do you know he left through the front?"

"Because I photographed him leaving in a car."

"How did you get back here?"

"I went through the theater and I'm leaving out this side."

"You're kidding us."

"I'm not kidding you. He's left. He's gone."

They didn't believe me; it was just like Richmond. I left them behind again.

Elvis learns about the latest air disaster as he and his group wait for a cab outside Pennsylvania Station, New York City. He preferred the train. Bill Black looks over his shoulder. July 1, 1956.

A devoted fan, who has waited hours for this moment, struggles to keep her composure outside the Hudson Theatre, site of the "Steve Allen Show." Accompanied by her father, she wept after Elvis left for rehearsal.

Rehearsing "You Ain't Nothin' But a Hound Dog"; the song had yet to be released as a single. The dog in the top hat is Allen's gag.

At an impromptu
conference be-
tween rehearsals,
Elvis fields ques-
tions from the
New York press.
They expected
a yokel but,
instead, found
a Southern
gentleman.

The Colonel gives
a reporter a story.

Preparing for
dress rehearsal:
Allen's solution to
circumventing
Elvis' controversial
physical style was
to put him in tails.

Tom Diskin,
seated, Colonel
Parker's right-
hand man.

Before Greek columns and blue sky, Elvis opens his appearance on the second national "Steve Allen Show" with "I Want You, I Need You, I Love You." July 1, 1956.

To a polite but enthusiastic response to his second number, "You Ain't Nothin' But a Hound Dog," Elvis strides out stage right.

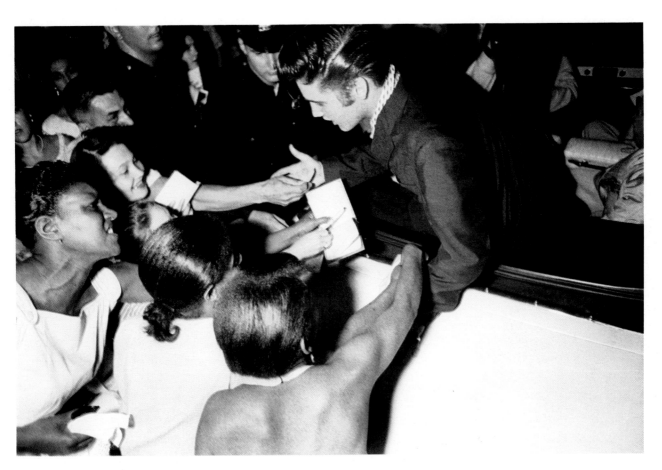

Elvis quickly
changes out of his
tails into his cow-
boy costume, as-
sisted by two
NBC dressers.
This was live
televison.

The show's over.
Outside the en-
trance to the Hud-
son Theatre, Elvis
receives his fans
for a moment be-
fore he is taken
away.

Studio One
"Let's try it again."

At eleven on Monday morning, a Checker cab left me at 155 East Twenty-fourth Street, a six-story building that was headquarters for RCA Victor. The high-fashion glamour of noiseless carpeting, designer lighting and cosmopolitan receptionists had not yet glossed the lobbies of the recording industry. What distinguished this paneled, linoleum-floored room from any other industrial haven was the sculpted logo hanging behind the front desk — a big white mutt with his nose in an Edison phonograph.

Past a pair of swinging doors was a long hall lit by fluorescent lights with telephone booths and vending machines. To the right, a single door opened onto a small reception area with a coffee table, a few standing ashtrays, leather chairs and a small group of recording people. On the far side of this room was an exposed platform that supported the engineering console and the recording equipment.

A mono speaker was suspended over the door. Before the reception area and to the right of the engineering console, a wide, double-glass window looked onto Studio 1, where I could see Elvis, his musicians, the Jordanaires and, sitting in a corner, Junior Smith.

Of the several people in the reception area, I recognized only Anne Fulchino, the woman responsible for my being there, and Steve Sholes, head of the Country and Western Artist and Repertoire division. Neither the Colonel nor Tom Diskin were present.

I set down my lighting gear, greeted Anne, nodded to the engineer and his assistant and introduced myself to Mr. Sholes. Steve was a big man with a gentle manner and a dedicated brow, a twenty-year veteran in the music business and a man whose ear had picked up on artists like Chet Atkins and Hank Snow. Steve had been instrumental in signing Elvis with RCA. My introduction was more than professional courtesy. In order for me to shoot freely I had to get people accustomed to my presence.

The studio looked like a set from a 1930's science fiction movie. It was a large rectangular space of acoustical tile walls ribbed with monolithic half cylinders. These ran vertically on the long sides of the rectangle and horizontally on the short sides. The high ceiling was rippled with more parallel cylinders and two pipes of fluorescent light. The floor was a series of short strips of wood scaled in a sawtooth pattern of right angles. In the center of the room lay a patch of carpet on which the musicians had placed their instruments.

The assistant engineer placed mikes and said "test" to the engineer. D. J. "Sticks" Fontana tightened his drumheads, tapping and booming. Bill Black plumbed his bass. Scotty Moore tuned his guitar. Shorty Long played the piano. Elvis joined the Jordanaires in a spiritual. I took a few pictures and when they stopped for a break, I said good morning. Elvis, eyes bright and generous, asked me, "How ya feel?"

"A little tired. It should be a good session today."

I had no reason to believe it one way or the other. He just cocked his head like John Wayne surveying the cattle drive and said, "Well, I hope so."

Steve walked in and suggested they record "Hound Dog" first. While Elvis and Steve conferred in a corner, the engineer set the levels.

Recording in those days did not enjoy the luxury of twenty-four-track tape recorders and postrecording mixes. Modern artists can add or subtract instruments, overdub, change levels, and electronically alter the sound with so much range that the final product may barely resemble what was heard at the original session. Nineteen fifty-six was still in the era of monaural sound. The engineer ran single-track tape recorders and mixed the sounds as they were recorded. The entire process was restricted to the present: if it wasn't right from the beginning you had to stop and do it all over again. Patching separate takes together wouldn't do. The only way the musicians and singers knew what they sounded like was to perform a rehearsal take and listen to the playback. What the engineer heard at the moment of recording was what you got.

After a cold but punchy rendition in the studio (where the sound seemed so lopsided at times that I could barely hear Elvis over the drums), everyone sat on the floor around the one speaker in the room. Elvis held his forehead in his hand and con-

centrated on the sound. Steve Sholes stood by, shirt sleeves rolled up, his hands in his pockets, waiting for the reaction.

At the end of the playback, Elvis looked up preoccupied and discontent. The engineer was concerned the drums were too loud. Elvis thought they were all right, he wanted more guitar and another run-through.

The second mix was satisfactory. Steve resumed his position in the control booth. The engineer cued, "Hound Dog, take one."

Elvis began, "You ain't nothin' but aaah-oooh, let's try it again."

"Okay, anytime you're ready, we're still rolling. Take two."

A word stuck in his throat. "Take three."

Elvis opened, didn't like the way it sounded, and tried again. "Take four."

He got past the opening. As the rhythm overtook his body, he jerked and bounced, driving the beat into the music. Steve interrupted, "Elvis, we're going to have to try it again." Instead of cueing the engineer, Steve walked out of the booth and crossed over to Elvis. Calmly, he said, "You went off-mike." Elvis nodded. It looked as if they had had this problem before. "Take five" . . . .

His voice cracked, the drums were too loud, somebody hit a microphone, he went off-mike again. When the musicians blew it, they jokingly made it worse. Scotty fluffed a note and then slid into a completely different riff. D. J. missed a beat and plummeted into a pirouetting drumroll. Elvis in reply mocked the lines, "Ain't no friend of mi-ine?"

At around take fourteen, I stopped taking pictures. The humor that had started the session was fading and people began glancing at Elvis to check his mood. He wasn't happy. Out of seventeen takes, maybe four were complete. Not a very good record, considering the routine of a good cut after seven or eight takes which I had observed with other singers.

Elvis didn't lose his temper and he didn't look for a scapegoat. At other RCA recording sessions, sometimes I had become the excuse. "I can't concentrate with the photographer here." It didn't matter that I was crouched in some corner trying to look like a piece of furniture. It was still my fault.

Elvis was unique. In his own reserved manner he

kept control, he made himself responsible. When somebody else made a mistake he sang off key. The offender picked up the cue. He never criticized anyone, never got mad at anybody but himself. He'd just say, "Okay, fellas, I goofed."

Elvis turned away from the mike to face the wall and shook the tension from his body, jerking his arms, twisting his torso, craning and bobbing his head. When he turned back to the microphone, he ran his hands through his hair, and in a low, determined voice said, "All right, let's try it."

Take eighteen. Elvis closed his eyes, took a deep breath and grated into the microphone, grabbing the lyric and spiking it with a nastiness that made it bite. Scotty's guitar found its edge and Bill's bass surged with the momentum they had been missing. By the end of the take, the Jordanaires thought they had it.

Elvis wanted to try it again. At take twenty-six, Steve thought they had it. Elvis still thought he could do it a little better. Four takes later, Steve called over the PA, "Okay, Elvis. I think we got it." They had engaged the law of diminishing returns. Mistakes were creeping in. Elvis rubbed his face, swept back his hair and resigned. "I hope so, Mr. Sholes."

The working relationship at this session was a departure from what I had seen at other recording sessions. Other artists I had covered were directed by a producer. He was the man in charge, and often the atmosphere was formal and businesslike. With Elvis the mood was casual, relaxed, joking. Steve did not dictate, he managed. And though Elvis was not a forward, take-charge character, he was clearly the one who had to be pleased. When it concerned his music, no one was more serious.

The recording had taken over two hours and without the air conditioner turned on (the mikes would have picked up the noise), the air in the room hung low and close. The double doors were opened, admitting cool air, the noise of vending machines and visitors with glowing compliments. Elvis combed his hair, drank the Coke offered by Junior and shrugged in reply to comments about how good the music was. Steve trod lightly: "Elvis, you ready to hear a playback?" As if bad news never had good timing, he said, "Now's as good a time as any."

Elvis sat cross-legged on the floor in front of the speaker. The engineer announced the take over the PA and let the tape roll. Elvis winced, chewed his fingernails and looked at the floor. At the end of the first playback, he looked like he didn't know whether it was a good take or not. Steve called for take eighteen.

Elvis pulled up a folding chair, draped his arms across its back and stared blankly at the floor. As his voice pierced the speaker grille, everyone waited for his reaction. Then, as if he had received a telegram bearing news that, yes, there's good rockin' tonight, he popped his head up and cracked a smile. Take eighteen was a contender.

The engineer racked take twenty-eight. Elvis left his chair and crouched on the floor, as if listening in a different position was like looking at a subject from a different angle. Again he went into deep concentration, absorbed and motionless. For someone who had to wring the music from his body, he sure took it back lying down. At the end of the song, he slowly rose from his crouch and turned to us with a wide grin, and said " This is the one."

While Junior took orders — turkey on rye, chicken salad, don't forget the apple pie, Pepsi, Coke — I picked up my lunch from the machines: a Hershey bar with nuts, another pack of Viceroys and a cup of coffee. I needed to stretch my legs so I wandered into the lobby.

Looking through the front door I saw three grammar-school girls watching two high-school girls standing vigil against the wall of the doorway. The teenagers wore skirts, and placards pasted with Elvis photos which read: "We want the gyratin' Elvis" and "We want the real Elvis." I stepped outside and took their picture.

I asked them, "Hi, where you from?"

"We came in from Brooklyn this morning."

"What are the signs for?"

"You saw the show last night, didn't you?"

"What was the matter?"

"Elvis was too tame. They kept him from moving and we didn't like it. We want to see Elvis move and we don't care if our parents don't like it. We want to see the real Elvis. Please, tell him what we think, okay?"

"When I see him, I'll tell him. Good luck."

"Goodbye."

I left them as I found them, standing at attention with their backs against the wall.

In the studio Elvis, D. J., Scotty and Bill sat near the piano eating their sandwiches, glad that the morning session was over and that it had turned out well, talking about how good it would be to get back to Memphis, yeah, Memphis, see the folks and relax. As I set up some lighting gear, I heard something about a Russwood concert on the Fourth of July. I asked them how they were getting down to Memphis. D. J. told me they were taking the 11:30 A.M. train out of Pennsylvania Station the following morning.

Junior collected the lunch garbage. Steve came in with a stack of demonstration records ("demos") the size of small albums, with sheet music for each tucked into the record jackets. Elvis looked at the titles and handed three to Steve who handed them to the engineer. Then he sat back, hands behind his head, looked at the rolling ceiling and listened.

The demos were straightforward renditions without much style but with lyrics that were sung clearly and audibly. "Anyway You Want Me" was followed by a song written by Otis Blackwell.

When it ended, Elvis said, "Let me hear 'Don't Be Cruel' again. Somethin' I like about that one." As they played it again, Elvis gathered the sheet music, withdrew to the speaker area and faced the corner. With one hand leaning against the wall, he stood alone as though waiting for his baby's train that had long since gone. The song ended, "Baby, it's just you I'm thinking of." He came back and said, "That's the one I want to try."

Strumming his guitar with the sheet music still held in his hand, he quickly found the melody. By the time everyone gathered around the piano, he had already memorized the lyrics.

Elvis played his version on the keyboard to Shorty, who noted the changes on the sheet music, while the musicians played it for themselves and the Jordanaires harmonized a bebop.

The problem was the opening. Elvis asked Scotty, "Whaddya think?"

Scotty replied with his guitar, "Dum-dim-da-di-di-dum-dem."

Elvis thought it over and said "Try a little more space."

Scotty came back, "Dumm, demm, ba-di-da, dumm, demm, ba-di-da."

Elvis smiled. Steve raised an eyebrow. D. J. joined in slowly.

Elvis thought for a moment and said, "D. J., come in behind Scotty and slow it down a little." Hoyt Axton of the Jordanaires suggested a "Bop-Bop" at the end of each phrase and a "Wah-Wah" on the refrain, and in twenty minutes they had a version ready to go.

Elvis asked, "Whaddya think, Mr. Sholes?"

Steve replied, "Okay, Elvis, let's try it."

It was the first time I had seen material prepared at the recording session itself. The convention was that everyone arrived prepared to record. The choice of material was made beforehand and the musical arrangements written so that expensive studio time would be devoted to working out minor details.

After hearing the first rehearsal take, Steve said, "Sounds good to me. Want to go for a take?" Elvis answered directly, "No, I wanna try another rehearsal."

They tried it again. Elvis changed his interpretation from a bouncing bop to the more intimate, muted feeling of a lover deeply hurt. He was giving himself a choice.

As the two takes were cued up, Elvis was constantly moving, shifting, changing pace. He was not very talkative. Some people carried on nervous conversations. Elvis let his body move. Often the only way the musicians knew how well they were playing was by his mood and movements. Rapidly changing movements meant uncertainty. A glint in the eye meant good. A flashing smile said great.

After listening to the two rehearsal takes, Elvis smiled with satisfaction and said, "Let's go for one." He didn't say which one, it wasn't necessary. The musicians and the Jordanaires knew their parts and it was up to Elvis to make any changes.

Without the interruptions caused by his rocking off-mike, there were a few short takes and the momentum of the music quickly gathered everyone into a joyous foot-tapping, finger-snapping spree. The band was tight and Elvis was loose. At take six, Steve, who was in the control room, nodded, and everyone knew they had it. Once he had a good rendition Elvis knew he could take a risk. He wanted to try a few more.

At the completion of take eight, Steve announced over the intercom, "That was very good, Elvis."

Elvis grinned, "Yeah, that felt good. Let's hear it."

It was late. The only noise in the hallway was the scratch of the janitor's broom. Elvis could have called it a day — they had recorded two sides of a single — but instead he wanted to try "Anyway You Want Me."

The engineer spun the demo. Elvis crouched again, his ear directly in line with the speaker. As he listened, he moved his hands as if he were molding clay.

Everyone resumed their positions for a single rehearsal, using the same microphone levels and arrangements with which they recorded "Don't Be Cruel." It was apparent that they were prepared. Elvis knew the lyrics and the band and the Jordanaires knew their parts. The playback brought a tired smile to Elvis' face.

Elvis arched his back, rolled his head, combed his hair. His soft round features had gained the stoic quality of heavy fatigue. Scotty waited, and when Elvis set the beat with a flagging hand, his guitar strained a melancholy wail. Elvis pleaded, he cajoled, he resigned, "In your hands my heart is clay, to take and mold as you may."

At the fourth take, Steve said they had it. Elvis said again, "That's fine, Mr. Sholes. Let's try it one more time." He was as relentless as his fans.

He took a chance. His voice cracked, then it broke. He became so fragile in his plea that you had to believe him. "Anyway you want me, that's how I will be." It was more than his voice that made the girls cry; he made them cry because he made them believe. "Yes, anyway you want me, well, that's how I will be, I will be." He walked away from the microphone exhausted, finished.

Before he left the studio, Elvis asked for an acetate record (a quick cut that could be made overnight) of the best take of each song. Steve said it would be delivered to him at the Warwick Hotel by morning.

The warm night air and city noise released the compression of a day that was spent inside a windowless room. It felt like I was standing on solid ground after a long drive.

The Buick convertible gleamed in the light from the post office across the street. As Elvis approached the car, he was greeted by some fans, not giggling teenaged girls, but postal workers, some of whom were twice his age.

"Hey, I saw you on the 'Steve Allen Show.' I really liked ya." The man speaking had a crew cut and wore a sleeveless shirt that revealed powerful arms. He pulled out a piece of paper from his back pocket.

"My daughter would really appreciate it, if I could get your autograph."

"Sure," said Elvis.

A thick man in thick glasses told him, "You know my wife really likes the way you sing. Could you sign one for her?"

"Yeah, sure."

After a few more autographs, Junior called, "Hey, Elvis, we gotta get back to the hotel."

Elvis waved good-bye. "Well, so long, fellas. Keep up the good work."

The workers enjoyed that one, saying, "Yeah, see ya around."

"So long, Elvis."

Elvis hopped into the back of the convertible and returned to the night.

Listening to a playback of "Anyway You Want Me" during a recording session in RCA Victor Studio One. Manhattan, July 2, 1956.

Recording "Don't Be Cruel." From left: D. J. Fontana, drums; Bill Black, bass; the Jordanaires, back-up vocals.

Elvis belts out "You Ain't Nothin' But a Hound Dog."

(Following page) Elvis, his musicians and the Jordanaires listen to another take of "You Ain't Nothin' But a Hound Dog." It took nearly thirty takes before Elvis was satisfied.

(Preceding page) Elvis withdraws to a corner of the studio to hear a new demo record by Otis Blackwell. The box at the left is the mono speaker. Song-writers commonly used the demo, in addition to sheet music, to submit their material. The song: "Don't Be Cruel."

After several takes
of "Don't Be
Cruel," Elvis listens
for the right cut
with his ears at
the same level as
the speaker.

Working out the arrangement (below) for "Don't Be Cruel." Left to right: D.J. Fontana (in the shadow), Gordon Stoker, Hoyt Hawkins, Neal Matthews, Jr. (obscured), Elvis.

(Following page) Left to right: unknown, D.J. Fontana, Neal Matthews, Jr., Joe Carlton, Steve Sholes, Carroll "Junior" Smith, Elvis, Scotty Moore. Steve Sholes, head of Country & Western Artist and Repertoire, talks with Joe Carlton, his boss at RCA Victor, during a lull in the recording session. Steve was instrumental in signing Elvis to an RCA Victor contract in November of 1955.

On The Train: New York to Memphis

"Are you Elvis Presley?"

At eleven-thirty Tuesday morning, on the eve of the Fourth of July, we caught a Pullman that was on its way to Washington, Chattanooga and points south. The conductor said we'd be in Memphis the following afternoon.

As we emerged from the tunnel under the Hudson River to the sunlight of industrial New Jersey, Elvis and Junior were unpacking in their compartment while Scotty, D. J. and Bill were moving into the compartments next-door. I was looking for the Colonel.

I found him and Tom Diskin in the restaurant car. The Colonel turned from the scenery and directed, like a drill instructor to a fresh boot, "Take a load off your feet, Wertheimer. Have a bite to eat."

"Yeah, I think I will, Colonel, but I'll sit here in case Elvis comes by."

"Okay. Suit yourself."

I took a seat at the table across the aisle and ordered a club sandwich, something I could eat with one hand, so I could be ready with the camera in the other.

Elvis walked in with Junior, dressed in the same grey suit and diamond point shirt he'd worn to the "Steve Allen Show." In fact, with the exception of the recording session, he'd been wearing a suit since Friday.

He looked over my sandwich and quipped, "I see photographers gotta eat, too."

I swallowed a half-chewed lump. "Yeah, eat while I can."

"Finger not tired, yet?"

I looked at my index finger and flexed it for him. He chuckled and said, "Good," and slouched next to Tom.

Junior carefully laid a white linen napkin on his lap and ordered a cup of coffee. Elvis asked for a club sandwich and a Coke. All sat quietly looking out the window. Newark, New Jersey, blurred by.

The Colonel turned to Elvis. Sounding like a father asking a son what he did at school today, he said, "How'd it go yesterday at the recording session?"

Elvis replied blandly. "It went pretty well."

The Colonel carried on the conversation. "The reaction was terrific on the "Steve Allen Show." Better than I thought."

Elvis shrugged. He seemed unimpressed. "Glad to hear it."

This appeared to be a routine. The Colonel would start the conversation and Elvis would end it.

"It's gonna be good to get back home. I'm sure your folks'll be mighty glad to see you," said the Colonel.

"Yeah, it'll be good to see 'em."

That was the end of the conversation. The Colonel looked out the window. Tom talked shop. Junior talked to Elvis, and Elvis ate his sandwich. It was two generations sitting at separate tables.

A teenaged blonde walked by, quickly backtracked and examined Elvis' profile. He let her have a good look, then turned and looked her straight in the eye. She retreated.

"Oh, excuse me, you look a lot like Elvis Presley."

With a straight face, he said, "Oh, do I?"

She shifted to view him from another angle. "Yes, you certainly do."

Without another thought, she walked away. Elvis smirked. Nobody else at the table paid any attention. It seemed as if they had seen this routine before.

The train passed through Baltimore and Washington. I left Elvis alone. It was going to be a long trip and I wanted to give him some room.

Outside Alexandria, I knocked on his open door. A porter plugged something into the shaver outlet then walked out. Elvis combed his hair.

"Hi, Elvis. Do you mind if I come in?"

It was all the same to him. "No, come on in." On his lap was a portable phonograph.

"I'm not disturbing you, am I?"

"No, not at all."

At his side was a pile of records in plain brown sleeves labeled "Soundcraft." He selected one and put it on. It was "Don't Be Cruel" on an acetate disc that had been cut the night before. As he listened, he ran a thumb across his lower lip and gazed at the scenery. I waited until the song was finished before I spoke.

"Elvis, I've got a question I want to ask you."

His eyes cleared. "Yeah, what is it?"

"Why do you play it back on such an inexpensive little record player when you can hear it in the studio over a great speaker system and really hear everything that's on the record."

"Well, you know, most of the people who buy my records can't afford expensive record players. I want to hear it the way they hear it. If it sounds good here, then I know it's good."

He thought a moment and added, "It's important that when I sing a song before an audience, I sing it the same way as I sang it on the recording."

He continued playing "Don't Be Cruel." After several run-throughs, he put on "Hound Dog," replaying certain parts over and over, listening with the same motionless concentration I had seen in the studio the day before. He repeated this routine with "Anyway You Want Me." When he finished playing his records for himself, he called in his musicians and his cousin. I left the compartment to allow them room.

While I watched the Virginia countryside, I thought about Elvis' consideration of his audience and how they heard his music. I was impressed.

I slept through Sweet Briar, Monroe, Lynchburg and dinner. When I checked on Elvis, he was already tucked in his berth, listening to his records in the company of a four-foot teddy bear held in the webbing at the foot of the bed. I took his picture. He put away his records, stared down my camera with boredom, rolled over and went to sleep.

Two doors down, Tom Diskin was typing on the stationery of "Thomas A. Parker." There was no "Colonel" attached to the letterhead. I wondered about his title but didn't bother to ask. I didn't want to touch on any sensitive areas.

I turned my camera toward Tom. He was a clean-cut man in his early thirties, with a soft-spoken, competent manner and a sober style quite the opposite of the good ol' boy glad-hand flamboyance of his Southern employer. Tom was from Chicago and he had a background in accounting. He took care of advance bookings, the box office receipts, letters, bills and any other loose ends the Colonel left unraveled.

When I took his picture, Tom told me I was wasting film. "I don't take good pictures." I said he was a handsome man but he didn't believe it. He just smiled and kept on typing.

The Colonel stepped in wearing his straw hat, black-framed glasses and a half-buttoned red-striped shirt. He looked like a football referee from the Panama Canal Zone. He lit the stogie clenched in his mouth and said to me, "Wertheimer, are you still at it? How can you take pictures, there's no light?"

"Well, it would help, Colonel, if you pushed your hat back a little bit. The light might hit some of your face."

The Colonel gladly obliged. He pulled the cigar out of his mouth, took off his glasses and removed his hat. He didn't bother to finish buttoning his shirt.

"Are you getting any good pictures?" he asked.

"Yeah, I'm getting good pictures, but my subject went to sleep, so I thought I'd hang around here for a while."

The Colonel waved his cigar. "Well, make yourself at home."

I took a seat across from the Colonel. He daubed his forehead with his handkerchief and fired another question. "You ever been down South?"

"Well, I was in Florida once."

"Then this is your first trip to Memphis."

"Yes, it is."

"Well, you're going to like it and you're going to see crowds like you never saw. If you think the other night at Richmond was something, wait 'til you see Russwood Stadium. You're going to see faces upon faces of people. That place is going to be packed."

"I'm looking forward to it."

In New York I had heard nothing but big bad wolf stories about the man. "Watch out for this guy, he's tricky," people said. Right now he was more like an uncle, sweet-talking and easygoing, and, besides, if it wasn't for him, I wouldn't be here. He could have dropped me at the last mail stop. So I took a chance.

"Colonel, I notice you rarely travel by Elvis' side. I know you're his manager but I never see you by his side unless it's some kind of business affair. Like yesterday, at the recording session, I assumed you were going to be there making all kinds of arrangements."

"When it comes to Elvis' music, he picks what he

wants to sing. I'm not a musician, I don't know about music. I know about handling acts and booking theaters. As far as traveling goes, I think it's a good idea that Elvis travels with people his own age."

"Is that why Junior is hanging around with Elvis all the time?"

"Junior is Mrs. Presley's sister's boy. Elvis feels more at ease with people his own age. I'm in my forties. They're in their twenties and that makes a big difference. But when it comes to deals, that's my job."

Tom pulled a letter out of the typewriter. The Colonel tried to light his cigar again. I took a picture and asked another question.

"Colonel, remember the other night in Richmond, at the Mosque Theatre?"

"What about it?"

"Well, after the first show, Elvis came out for an encore but after the second show, he left and didn't do an encore. How come?"

The Colonel thought about it, mouthed his unlit cigar and with the supreme confidence of an elder relating a law of nature, he said, "You know, Wertheimer, what you want to remember is . . . " — he said each word distinctly — "you always want to leave them a little hungry. That way you can be sure they'll come back for more."

The Colonel let me ponder his wisdom. Tom finished typing another letter and excused himself. I thought it was time to go. I was wrong.

"Wait a minute, Wertheimer."

The Colonel put his hat and glasses back on, refitted his cigar and took a seat at the typewriter. With a hunt and peck style, he labored through a letter. I took his picture. As I reset my frame, I noticed an addition to the bare compartment. In the corner of the window next to the typewriter, the Colonel had placed a pamphlet entitled, "Elvis Presley: why does he drive girls wild?" The Colonel didn't miss a trick.

I wondered if his typing was a "working" pose for my benefit, so I said "Colonel, you don't type very well. I know you're not a poor man. Why don't you have a secretary with you to type your letters? That way they'll be nice and neat and you won't have to sit there and hunt and peck."

The Colonel looked up startled. He slid the cold cigar to the side of his mouth and, with the conviction of a man who makes only sure bets, stated, "Wertheimer, I may not type very well but they *sure*

know what I mean up there."

"Up there" meant RCA in New York. I guessed that they did.

When I entered the restaurant car at six-thirty the next morning, the Colonel was reading his morning paper and drinking a second cup of coffee.

"Good morning, Colonel, how are you today?"

"Good morning, Wertheimer, see you made it. Sit down, have some breakfast."

He always called me "Wertheimer." He said it like a sergeant says "Atten-hut." The last time I had been known as "Wertheimer" was during my two-year stint in the army four years earlier. This time I didn't say, "Yes, sir." I said, "I think I will."

The Colonel pulled the paper in front of his face and continued to read. After the black waiter had taken my order, I looked over the front page. The headline of the *Knoxville Journal* declared "Integration Tied to School Bill." The secondary headline read "Hungary Declares Independence." It was July 4th.

I tried following the lead story but the Colonel lowered the newspaper so that he could peek over its top. He was about to say something but, instead, quickly jerked the paper up in front of his face and whispered a command.

"Wertheimer."

"Yes, Colonel?"

"Listen to me. Ask me a question, any question but just call me Colonel and say it loud. Now."

With a full voice appropriate to addressing a chief of staff, I declared,

"Uh, well, now, Colonel . . .

As I said "Colonel," I heard a snap behind me. Two crew-cut paratroopers in parade dress, their pants tucked into gleaming black boots, stood at attention with a smart salute. The Colonel dropped his paper, returned a casual salute and directed, "At ease, gentlemen, at ease. Have a good breakfast."

They answered in unison. "You, too, sir."

The troopers proceeded up the aisle to a table. I could see the light in the Colonel's eyes as he looked over the edge of the paper. His day had started out right. I didn't learn until later that the Colonel's title had not been earned in the armed forces but was an honorary title bestowed by the governor of Tennessee in 1953.

On his way out of the dining car, the Colonel took one more opportunity as he passed the paratroopers. "Enjoying your breakfast, gentlemen?"

"Yes, sir. Have a good morning, sir."

"You, too, ya hear."

We pulled into Chattanooga shortly after seven o'clock that morning. There was an hour left to kill before we changed to the day local to Memphis.

In the lobby of the train station, Elvis wandered over to the newspaper stand to survey the collection of men's magazines, comic books and movie pulps. *Modern Screen* caught his eye. Without saying a word to the two young women behind the counter, he brought the magazine across the lobby and borrowed a pen from Junior, who always had a shirt pocket full of pens, and wrote on a page in the middle.

On top of the stacks of candy bars, Elvis laid open the magazine to what was now an autographed story about himself. He turned and looked at me, as if to say, watch this. To the two women running the stand, he said, "That's for you." They looked at the photos, then at Elvis in his suit, white shirt and tie, and again at the photos. The woman at the cash register said, "Are you Elvis Presley?"

Elvis rubbed his hands together and said casually, "Yeah, I'm Elvis Presley. That's me."

He pointed to his pictures. They took turns looking curiously at the magazine while they served other customers. The woman at the register looked as if she didn't know whether to say thanks or ask for a quarter.

Elvis said, "You buy any of my records?"

She answered cautiously. "Yes."

He grinned. "That's nice. That's for you, honey."

She gave him a half-hearted thanks, still not convinced that he was Elvis Presley. Elvis nodded and walked away, happy that he had started his day right.

While Elvis finished his breakfast in the station coffee shop, the rest of us waited in the main lobby. A porter walked by. The Colonel rose from his seat, raised his cigar hand and called, "Eh, Portah? Portah?"

The porter, a tall black man in his forties, replied with grace. "Yassuh."

The Colonel reached his hand into his coat pocket and pulled out some bills. They were folded, so it was unclear how many dollars he held. Using the cash between his thumb and forefinger as a pointer, he instructed the porter.

"Portah, you see these bags here." The Colonel pointed his hand at some luggage near the bench.

"Yassuh."

"We're going on the eight o' clock train to Memphis and it should be here soon. Could you take these bags?"

"Yassuh."

"And there's some musical instruments out on that handcart on the platform." The Colonel pointed the money at the door. "And you'll see a teddy bear with them, a large teddy bear. Just make sure that they all get on that train."

"Yassuh."

"You do that now, ya hear?"

"Yassuh."

"And if you need some help, that's fine, you get some help."

"Yassuh."

The porter pulled over a small handcart, picked up the load of luggage and wheeled it out the door. The Colonel tucked the folded bills into his coat pocket.

A voice over the public address system garbled destinations. I heard Memphis announced. On the platform, Elvis, D.J., Junior and Bill gathered around Scotty and his pocket calendar and discussed upcoming dates. The number thirty-five day local to Memphis coasted in, and as Elvis climbed on first, I saw the Colonel marching up the platform with the porter at his side.

"Now, Portah, did you make sure that all of the luggage got on the train?"

"Yassuh. I got one o' the other boys ta help me."

"That's good. That's very good."

The Colonel mounted the car. The porter stood patiently on the platform. As he turned to face the porter, the Colonel reached into his coat pocket and, with a closed fist, laid the payoff in the grip of the porter's hand.

"Thank you, Portah."

When the porter unraveled the folded money, he discovered it was a single dollar bill. Saying "you" like it was a curse, he sarcastically replied, "Thank you, Suh."

The sarcasm was wasted on the Colonel. The porter shrugged it off and joined the other man who had been helping him.

I had heard that the Colonel was a man of his word. It seems he took that quite literally. He hadn't signed any contract with the porter.

Elvis spent the morning reading Archie comic books, looking out the window and combing his hair. At one point, tired of the comics, Elvis fidgeted and nervously pumped his leg. The conductor wandered by and asked him, "You nervous, son?" Elvis looked at him blankly and said, "Yes, sir."

After consuming two orders of Southern fried chicken picked up in Sheffield, Alabama, Elvis took a stroll with his teddy bear, a hefty panda the size of a chair. Halfway down the aisle, he found a couple of prospects. One was a brunette in a polka dot dress; the other was a blonde in a flower print. Both were in their early twenties. The blonde had his attention.

"Hi there, how are you?" Elvis asked her.

With the proper distance of a Southern lady, she replied, "We're pretty fine."

Elvis leaned on the seat in front of them and presented his furry friend. "I want you to meet my teddy bear."

She smiled politely and obliged, "Hello, teddy bear."

Elvis pressed on, as if he were the host of Romper Room and she was his guest. "Teddy would like to know your name."

She played along. "My name is Cindy Lou."

The brunette had been watching this exchange with a mild skepticism, looking as if she had heard some lines before, but this beat them all. Elvis turned his charm on her.

"What's your name?"

She answered matter-of-factly, "My name is Ann." Out of courtesy more than curiosity, Ann returned the question. "What's your name?"

"My name is Elvis."

Now she was curious. "Are you Elvis Presley?"

"Yeah, that's me."

"Really?"

"Yeah, there's a photographer."

That made it a fact. Ann didn't know what to do. "That's nice."

Elvis tried to move things along. "I'm going home to see the folks. We'll be doing a benefit tonight at Russwood Park. You going to Memphis?"

The blonde now spoke. "No, we'll be getting off before Memphis."

"Too bad you can't be there. It would be nice to see you."

"We sure would like to be there."

"Maybe I'll see you later."

They both smiled graciously and said good-bye.

Elvis wandered up the aisle with the teddy bear on his hip and took a drink from the water cooler.

As he walked back down the aisle, he held the teddy bear in front of him. As he passed the two women, he moved the teddy bear to his side, and like a ventriloquist with his dummy said, "Hi, y'all" as he breezed on. The brunette peeked around the seat to see if Elvis looked back. He didn't. The two giggled. It was hard to tell if they were laughing at him or his joke.

On the other side of Grand Junction, Tennessee, Elvis woke from a catnap. I was seated across from him, reading *Life* and keeping watch. The Colonel was across the aisle, an unlit cigar in his mouth, chatting with Tom.

It had been like musical chairs the entire trip. You had your seat as long as your body filled it. Otherwise, it was fair game, and at this point, I was in the seat the Colonel had occupied earlier.

Elvis got up and leaned over to me. With his eyes, he told me to keep quiet. He grabbed the Colonel's hat from the luggage rack above me and obscuring the hat with his body, sauntered past the Colonel into the hallway toward the lounge. I was ready for a soft-shoe number.

Wearing the hat at a rakish tilt, Elvis paraded down the hallway, exaggerating the Colonel's imperious drawl, "Now, y'all, y'all hear this. Now y'all make sure . . .

The Colonel didn't get it. He wasn't paying any attention. He was busy gabbing.

Elvis returned the hat. The Colonel interrupted himself, looked at the hat, realized it was his, stuck it on his head and carried on where he had left off. Elvis looked at me and threw his hands up. Better luck next time. I thought about suggesting a paratrooper outfit but kept it to myself.

At a stop in a rural suburb of Memphis that wasn't much more than a grass field turning yellow and a signpost that read "White," the Colonel let his boy go with a pat on the back and instructions to say hello to his Ma and to be good. Elvis swept his hair back and stepped off the train carrying only his records.

We pulled out in the direction of downtown Memphis. Elvis, still dressed in his suit and white knit tie, drifted through the burrs and foxtails, wondering which way to go. When he reached the sidewalk at the edge of the field, a black matron gave him directions. With a wave to us, and a smile that could be seen for a hundred yards, Elvis walked home alone.

(Preceding page)
Grand Con-
course, Pennsylva-
nia Station, New
York City, July 3,
1956. Destination:
Memphis.

En route to Mem-
phis, Elvis combs
his hair while a
porter plugs in the
portable phono-
graph Elvis
brought along to
play his new
recordings.

During the first afternoon of a long train ride, Elvis played his new records over and over again. The discs were quick-cut acetates made after the recording session.

Listening to the previous day's work one more time before going to sleep, his teddy bear keeping him company. The record player is sitting on a ledge to the right of his berth.

While Elvis is asleep, the Colonel poses for a picture before lecturing Wertheimer, the novice, on the finer points of show biz.

Tom Diskin, the Colonel's lieutenant. (Far right) July 4, 1956. The first to rise, the Colonel enjoys his morning newspaper and a second cup of coffee.

A late riser having breakfast alone at the Chattanooga train station. Bacon and eggs, toast and jelly, no coffee. Milk washed it all down.

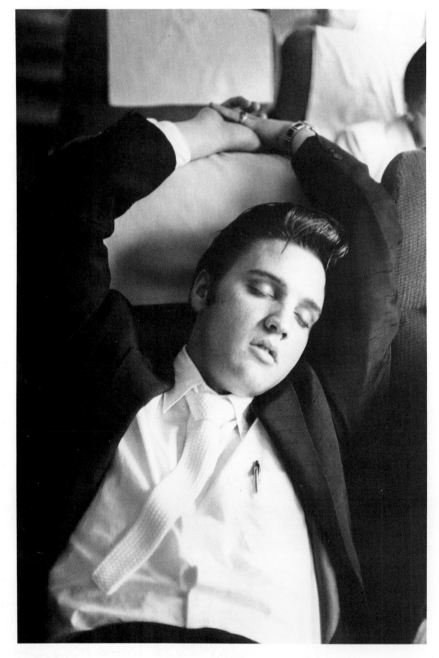

On the day
local out of
Chattanooga,
which made all
the stops. Every
one.

"Junior" Smith naps with the panda while Elvis studies an "Archie" comic book.

(Following page) Lunchtime, Sheffield, Alabama. Elvis waits his turn for a double order of Southern fried chicken, milk and "Hostess" cupcakes.

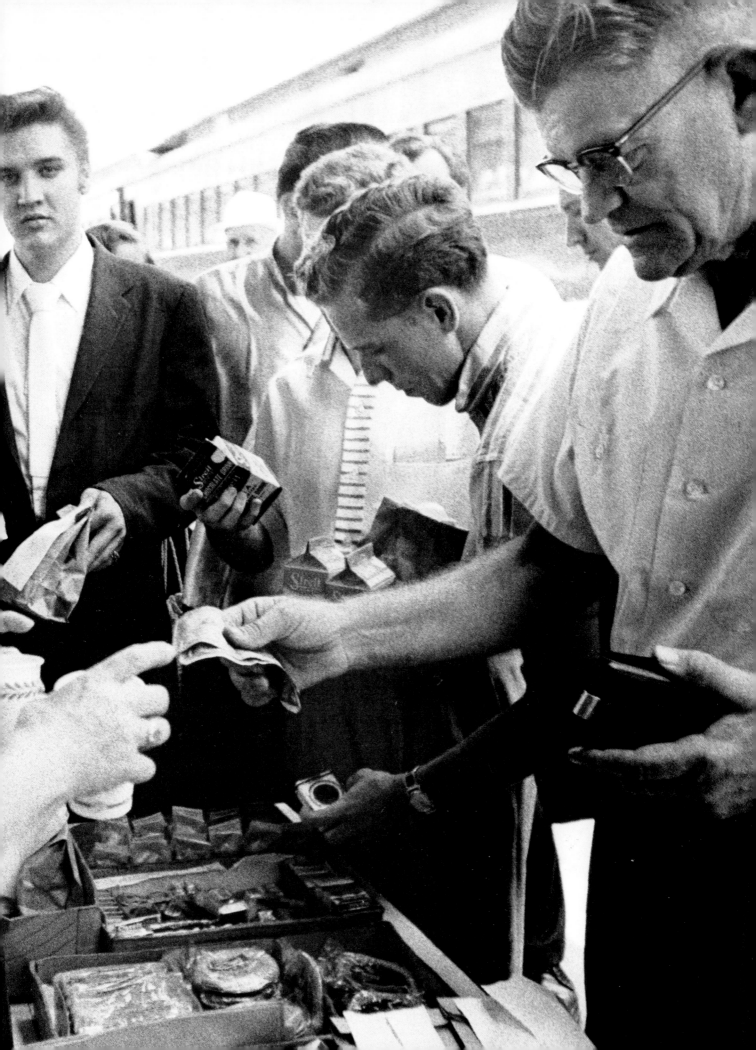

Colonel Parker
and friend.

Lunch was the last
meal Elvis had be-
fore his 10:00 P.M.
appearance that
night at Russwood
Stadium in Mem-
phis.

As he approached home, Elvis tucked his shirt in, straightened his tie, combed his hair and washed his hands. There weren't any paper towels.

Home

"I'm gonna show you what the real Elvis is like tonight."

1034 Audubon Drive was a postwar suburban home that could have been built for any GI-made-good anywhere in the country. The late afternoon sun highlighted a typical American house: pastel green board-and-batten siding, slate-grey tiled roof, red brick trim, white windows decorated with black shutters and a black ranch-style front door. A freshly cut lawn grew from the sidewalk to the front door, which looked rarely used. No well-worn path ran to the front porch. The occupants were as recent as the hedge saplings in the brick planter on the face of the house.

There were no picket fences or brick walls. It was a neighborhood of family homes and manicured lawns whose only boundaries were driveways and trees.

On the left side of the house was a carport sheltering two late model Cadillacs, one pink, one white, and a crowd: young mothers with babies in diapers, little girls with flowers in their hair, local boys and young women dressed in their best.

I edged by the gathering toward the side door. A graceful young blonde in a white dress answered my ring and invited me into the kitchen. Elvis had changed from his coat and tie into a collarless shirt and motorcycle cap. He had his arms around a stout woman in a baggy housedress. Her features, round and soft from age, deepened her eyes.

The blonde closed the door and quietly stepped aside. I greeted Elvis. He looked at me and said, "Ma, this is the photographer I was telling you about who was up in New York with me."

"How do you do, Mrs. Presley."

In a subdued, kind voice, she said, "Come in."

I thanked her, set my gear down and returned to my range finder. It was a family kitchen. Doors of the veneered cabinets were ajar, the formica counters were cluttered with cereal bowls and drinking glasses. Elvis rolled up his sleeves and said, "Ma, I'm going out. I'm gonna drive around a little on my motorcycle."

Gently, she said, "You be careful now."

He put his arm around her, and said in the voice of assurance that every boy has used on his mother, "It's, okay, ma. I'm a big boy."

She fiddled with something in her hands. "Are you sure you don't want something to eat?"

"No, ma, I'm not hungry."

"Well, if you do, just let me know."

"I'll see you later."

Elvis gave the blonde a good-bye kiss on the lips and went out the door to the backyard. His mother addressed me. "Would you like something to drink? A glass of milk or some soda?"

"No, thank you. I would just like to put my camera bag somewhere."

She directed me to the den, a ranch-style room with a beamed stucco ceiling, dark wooden walls, venetian blinds and an odd mixture of Victorian and 1950's overstuffed furniture. It looked like the catchall for what didn't fit in the rest of the house. On a card table next to a standing ashtray was a portable phonograph buried under a litter of record jackets and notebooks. Newspapers filled a metal rack. A sewing table supported potted plants and paper bags. The walls held a plastic kitchen clock, a corncob pipe, a set of longhorns and Elvis' high school diploma. For "having sustained a correct moral deportment," L. C. Humes High School had "entitled" Elvis Aron Presley to a "testimonial" on the third of June 1953.

Mrs. Presley showed me a corner for my stuff. I wanted her to know I was interested in her son. "You know, Mrs. Presley, I've been with Elvis for the last few days and he's a very interesting young man. He kind of runs you ragged though. He's always doing something."

"Yes, he is a little nervous."

"Oh, I don't mean nervous. He's just always busy."

"Well, he has a lot to do."

She escorted me to the living room, a showcase of popular contemporary design: wide, thick chairs overlaid with bamboo leaves or tumbling ferns, blond split-level tables, a blond hi-fi console, more brass standing ashtrays, two television sets (another was in the den) and white drapes splotched with some abstract design borrowed from Joan Miró. Scattered around were stuffed animals: tigers, monkeys, bears, dogs.

Hanging on the blond paneled wall next to the drapes was an oil copy of the "collector's edition" publicity photo, a dreamy Elvis with his cheek resting against his clasped hands, his lips full, his eyes looking intimately at the viewer. A lamp was attached to the top of the gilt frame.

All the other frames on the wall were his awards. These were what his mother wanted me to see. There was a Cash Box Award of 1955 for the "Most Promising Up and Coming Country Male Vocalist," a Disc Jockey Award from *Billboard* for being "Most Promising," also 1955, a *Billboard* Triple Crown Award for "Heartbreak Hotel" and finally, the big money, his first gold record, awarded in April 1956. The excitement of a mother's pride lifted her deep eyes and, for a moment, gave Gladys Presley a joyful youth she seemed to have missed.

In the backyard, which was a ranging field bordered by a thick stand of trees at its rear, a swimming pool was being filled with a garden hose. From the brick patio, I saw the three-foot-high fence of the carport contain more than thirty people. They were watching Elvis, who was jumping up and down in the midst of another group on the far side of the yard.

He couldn't start the motorcycle. A chubby friend straddled the front wheel of the Harley to keep it steady, holding on to the handlebars and pressing his belly into the headlight. Elvis jumped on the starter again. No luck. He kept trying until his shirt stuck to his back, and when he finally took a breather he said, "Some days, things just don't go right."

The girls who were standing by, all dressed up and holding their purses and Brownie cameras seized the opportunity for some autographs. The boys looked exasperated, as if they had business to take care of. Elvis had to get a motorcycle started, why are you bothering the man with this stuff? As far as the girls were concerned, they couldn't care less. They didn't want their man going anywhere.

A man in a checked shirt and dark slacks crossed the grass. His handsome face with square jaw and high forehead under blond wavy hair made him look younger than his years. He was about the Colonel's age but without his weight. His name was Vernon Presley.

He said, "Having problems, son?"

"Yeah, Daddy. Daddy, can you get me a wrench?"

After Elvis had given a few autographs, his dad arrived with the wrench, got down on his hands and knees and took care of the problem. Elvis kicked it over and the engine popped into motion.

The carport crowd commented "doesn't he look good" and "doesn't he look healthy" as Elvis wheeled the bike out of the driveway. He signed some more autographs, took on a young boy as passenger and rapped down the street. Ma kept vigil.

When he returned, I asked him, "Elvis, how about taking me for a ride around the block and then I can get some pictures of you in action?"

He didn't hesitate. "Hey, that's a good idea. I like that."

I handed my second camera and spare film to the young boy as I took his place on the back.

The city block I had in mind turned out to be a country mile. While we shot down the road, Elvis pointed out the sights. I couldn't pay any attention, I was trying to hold on to my camera with one hand and my life with the other. I looked at the speedometer. It read "50." Riding in a car moving at fifty miles an hour doesn't seem that fast but, on a motorcycle, it feels like a hundred.

"Elvis, can you slow down a little bit?" I asked.

"Going too fast for ya?"

"It's jiggling the camera."

We slowed down, but not because I asked. The motor started coughing, and then it died. We coasted to the side of the road in front of a few isolated storefronts closed for the Fourth of July. There wasn't a gas station in sight.

Elvis walked to the dividing line and looked up and down the road. I was more concerned than he was. I had run out of film and was enraged at myself for losing the great "running out of gas" story.

"Elvis, what do we do?"

"Don't worry about a thing."

"Whaddya mean don't worry about a thing. You're out of gas. You want me to go and get some gas? Tell me where the gas station is and I'll bring some back."

"Just sit tight and don't worry about a thing."

He stood by the side of the road. A few cars drove by. Then a Chevy slowed down and pulled up next to the motorcycle. The driver was a young woman with her five-year-old girl. Elvis tipped his cap, leaned on the driver's window, looked into her eyes, and in a drawl, sweet and soft, he said, "Ma'am, I'm outta gas. Would you be kind enough to bring some back?"

I couldn't tell if she recognized him or not. She just nodded and drove off. I was a bit skeptical.

"Elvis, how do you know she's going to come

back?"

"She'll be back."

"But how do you know?"

"I know."

I couldn't say much to that. All I could do was watch Elvis kick pebbles.

Minutes later, she arrived with a yellow jerry can. If this was Southern hospitality, I was impressed. My city-wise suspicion had informed me that she would never be back.

Elvis met her halfway, took the can without uttering a word and emptied it into the tank. With my handkerchief, he wiped off the gas that spilled on the paint job. She held the can while he jumped on the Harley and started it.

Letting the motorcycle idle, he took her hand and escorted her to the car, explaining, "I gotta get back to the house, some people are waiting for me." He kissed her cheek. I thought he was a little too forward but she received it as only natural. As she got behind the wheel, Elvis walked around the car and kissed the little girl. They waved goodbye and drove away. I thought they deserved more than a good-bye kiss.

"Elvis, I could have given her some money."

"Don't worry about it. It's okay, she didn't want any money. She wouldn't have taken it anyway."

When we returned to the house, Elvis' mother was waiting at the edge of the driveway. Concerned that her son might have been splattered on the highway, she asked what happened. Elvis' explanation was direct and to the point, "We ran out of gas," and without another word, he drove into the carport with the crowd trailing behind. He didn't waste words with his mother, either.

The warm afternoon air lay still under a ninety-degree weight. Mother and grandmother relaxed under an umbrella on the patio. Little girls sat on the edge of the pool apron watching the boys play in water that was shallow because the pump didn't work and the garden hose was slow. A small group of teenagers viewed the backyard play from the shade of the carport.

Since I had arrived, the carport had become the fans' designated area, and though they were well-behaved, they were steadfast. The Presleys' calmly accepted this constant audience.

Elvis trotted out in his trunks, dove into the pool and, as soon as he surfaced, was tackled by one of his young mates. Elvis pushed him away. "Bobby wait a minute, hold it, don't." Bobby recoiled, his hands against his chest. Elvis shook the water from his arm. He had forgotten to take off his watch.

Instead of leaving the pool and drying off the watch with the towel he had tossed at its side, he yelled for his mother. Mrs. Presley promptly left her chair on the patio and scurried down the grassy incline.

"What is it, son?"

"Ma, I left my watch on."

He removed his watch and met his mother at the edge of the pool. Bobby and a couple of boys gathered round to await the verdict. As she examined the watch, Elvis asked, "Ma, is it still working?"

"I'll see, son."

She dried it off with her dress and held it to her ear. "I think it'll be fine son. I'll take care of it."

Elvis let out a rebel yell, splashing and wrestling his younger playmates with glee. In the three-foot-deep water they all looked like kids who had just discovered a watering hole. It was the first time I had seen him really relax.

When Dad tested the water, Elvis invited him to join the fun. "Come on, Dad."

Dad shook his head. "Not right now, son."

While the boys pounced on Elvis, Dad wandered to the edge of the pool and stood alone, treading his hands slowly through the cold water.

Elvis in his swimming pool was a good picture story for the fan magazines, so I borrowed a swimsuit from Mrs. Presley and waded in with the camera. Everybody carried on like I was just another relative taking snapshots.

From the pool, the center of activity moved to the den. The kids milled around waiting for the next event. Elvis took a phone call. The only phone in the house was located in the hallway that led to the bathroom and the bedrooms. It was placed at the bottom of a shelf rack that was a landing area for odds and ends: old newspapers, a spare light bulb, an empty candy box, a plastic red phone body studded with rhinestones and a photo album.

Dad was in the bathroom shaving, the door wide open. When I took his picture, he said, "But I got shaving cream on."

I told him it was all right. He rinsed off his razor and smiled, "Well, if that's what you want, okay."

Elvis hung up. Ma gave her boy a fresh pair of jockey shorts, and in return, he gave her a kiss on each cheek.

While Elvis was in the shower, I asked his mother if I could photograph the family album. The possibil-

ity that the family pictures might be spread from coast to coast didn't seem to faze her. It was "go right ahead if you want to." She was just being polite, but I wondered how a house this open could remain a home.

As I finished recording the family snapshots, I heard "Don't Be Cruel" coming from the living room. Elvis was leaning on the hi-fi console, bare-chested, in only his pants and socks, hair still tangled from the shower.

Across the room, his grandmother, Minnie Presley, sat deep in the couch, craning her head forward to make out the words. Next to her, a young lady perched on the edge of the couch, both hands holding her purse on her knees. She was a model of gentility in a blue polka dot white dress and polished black pumps. Curly brown hair drawn into a bun framed a noble face of teardrop eyebrows, intelligent eyes and tight red lips that restrained a kind smile. She was pert, prim and polite. Her name was Barbara. She could have been a schoolmistress.

Elvis, on the other hand, looked like the unruly student who spent most of his time leering at the teacher. "Let's dance," he said.

The lady demurred. "No, not now."

Elvis persisted as if he were trying to charm a first date into more than a good night kiss.

"Come on. It's okay."

To make sure that it was all right, Minnie excused herself, saying she had to get ready for the concert.

Elvis took the lady's hand and began dancing in the narrow lane between the coffee table and the couch. She went through the motions, and when she knew Elvis understood her heart wasn't in it she told him she just wanted to listen.

He shrugged, plopped down on the plush chair and sulked. She sat on the edge of the ottoman next to the hi-fi, picked at her pearl-clustered earrings and stared at the carpet. Elvis stared at her, clamped his lips in a pout and glared at a different patch of the carpet. His record filled the room, "Don't make me feel this way, come on over here and love me."

By the time the song was over, he had forgotten she'd been cruel. He wanted her approval. "How do you like it?"

"I think it's very good. I like it."

That made him happy. Instead of being the forward promoter that he was with his fans, he modestly offered, "Do you want to hear the other song?"

She answered yes.

He put on "Anyway You Want Me," and as she stood with her arms folded, Elvis gathered her against his bare chest in an awkward embrace. I figured I'd been a fifth wheel long enough, so I wandered back to his bedroom and committed it to posterity.

His bedroom had more color than Technicolor Cinemascope. On pastel yellow wallpaper speckled with blue and orange hung leaping ceramic minstrels on black oval plaques. White quilted bedspreads printed with pink and blue flowers covered the twin beds and overflowed into rose satin trim. Blue puppies rested against the blond headboards of the twin beds. And all I had was black and white film.

It was time to get ready for the concert. While a friend tuned Elvis' guitar, Dad and Elvis were in the bedroom closet trying to decide on which tie he should wear. The decision was red, the only color in his entire outfit, which was a black shirt in a shiny black suit that could have stopped them on the corners of Little Italy.

In the hallway, I saw the silhouette of a hat and cigar. The Colonel filled the doorway, crossed the threshold with a hortatory "how ya doin'" and took control.

A black and white sedan waited in the dark with a crowd of mothers and fathers, young boys and girls. As Elvis walked from the kitchen door to the police car, the oldest of the girls, who was on the verge of becoming a teenager, blurted out, "Elvis, I think you're wonderful and I love you."

Elvis acted natural. He caressed her hair, looked her square in the eye and spoke to her as though she were the only one. "That's real sweet of you, honey. Sure makes me feel good."

It made her feel better, so good she couldn't move.

Amid shouts of "Good luck" and "We're with you," Elvis climbed into the front seat and was soon squeezed in by a patrolman on his left and the Colonel on his right. I took the rear.

The police car cruised through the warm suburban night. Inside the radio squawked instructions to faraway patrols. Like the manager of a prizefighter, the Colonel asked his boy how he felt. Elvis said that he felt good, he felt fine, he was glad to be here, but he was concerned about the folks. He wanted to make sure they were going to get good seats. The Colonel told him Tom was taking care of it and not to worry about a thing.

They sat silently, cramped in the front seat watching the streetlights flash by. The cop added a note of reassurance.

"The place is packed. In case there's a problem, we've got enough boys from the sheriff's department and we've got the Shore Patrol."

What was the Shore Patrol doing in Memphis?

Russwood Park was packed. Banks of arc lights lit up thousands of people who covered the infield, left field, center field, right field and all the seats beyond; the throng seemed infinite as it swelled beyond the light into the shadows. The Colonel's prediction was right. It was faces on faces.

The sedan crept down the left field line and parked next to a tent that was pitched just outside third base. An immense bandstand trimmed with red, white and blue bunting filled the lane between third base and home plate.

The officer turned off the headlights and gripped the steering wheel. Elvis remained in the police car, tapping his fingers on the roof of the car while the Colonel left to instruct Tom Diskin at the tent.

The family party of Mom and Dad, Minnie, Barbara and a few relatives arrived and were escorted by Tom to some empty folding chairs beyond the far side of the bandstand. On the near side, next to the tent, the Jordanaires and Elvis' musicians tried to hear themselves above the sounds of the Bobby Morris Orchestra on stage.

It was past 10:30 P.M., and if the posters in the park were right, all these people had endured the heat and some procession of acts since eight o'clock that evening. No wonder they were restless. When the emcee told them Elvis was on his way, the restlessness quickly escalated into a chair-shifting, neck-stretching anticipation. A legion of deputies and sailors propelled Elvis to the stage, the master of ceremonies announced, "Here he is," and there he was, the deliverer, slicked and shiny black, taking possession of the stage with supreme confidence, releasing a tremendous roar with the power of a shock wave.

Waving all around, he cruised back and forth across the stage, feeling the place that was his, and before he returned to the center, he saluted his family as he stood at the edge of the stage.

After the first wave passed, the emcee presented Elvis with a scroll, in appreciation of his donation to a worthy local charity. (The entire concert was a benefit performance.) Elvis modestly claimed that it was really his honor to sing for this wonderful audience. And when the applause faded into silence, he let them know, he let them know this one was going to be his way. "I'm gonna show you what the real Elvis is like tonight."

He did. He sang hard and soft, fast and loose, the way he wanted it, ripping from "Mystery Train" to "I Got A Woman" to "Blue Suede Shoes"and to "Heartbreak Hotel." When he walked away from the mike, drenched in sweat, his hair in his eyes and his legs rubbery, they cried, they screamed, but they didn't charge. An act of faith kept them from crossing over.

It was fulfilled. He came back, and in defiance of all the lines that had been drawn, he howled "You ain't nothing but a hound dog," breaking any restraints that still survived, sending fourteen thousand people to the white-hot tip of a Fourth of July sparkler.

Elvis burned out at the edge of the stage, took a bow, waved good-bye and was quickly enveloped by a phalanx of policemen. The crowd roared and rushed the stage, but before they could overtake him, his guardians had dispatched him in a police car and returned him to the night.

As soon as the Colonel knew his boy was safe, he tore open a package and barked, "Here, get your Elvis photographs. Get your souvenir photographs."

They went like hundred dollar bills for a dime.

Having made his pocketful of dimes, the Colonel, speaking in a Southern drawl considerably thicker than his accent in New York, thanked the sheriff's deputies for their cooperation and after shaking their hands, climbed into the passenger seat of a station wagon. Tom took the wheel. I was crammed into the back with boxes of photos and souvenir programs. On the way to the motel, I looked them over.

"Colonel, how come there's no price marked on any of these programs?"

The Colonel pulled the unlit cigar out of his mouth and looked down the road as he gave me his last words of advice.

"Wertheimer, you never want to put a price on anything. In Vegas, we might sell them for two dollars. Here, we sell them for a dime. People only appreciate something they pay for. If you give it to them for nothing, it won't be appreciated."

He was just looking out for his boy's best interests. I never got close to Elvis again.

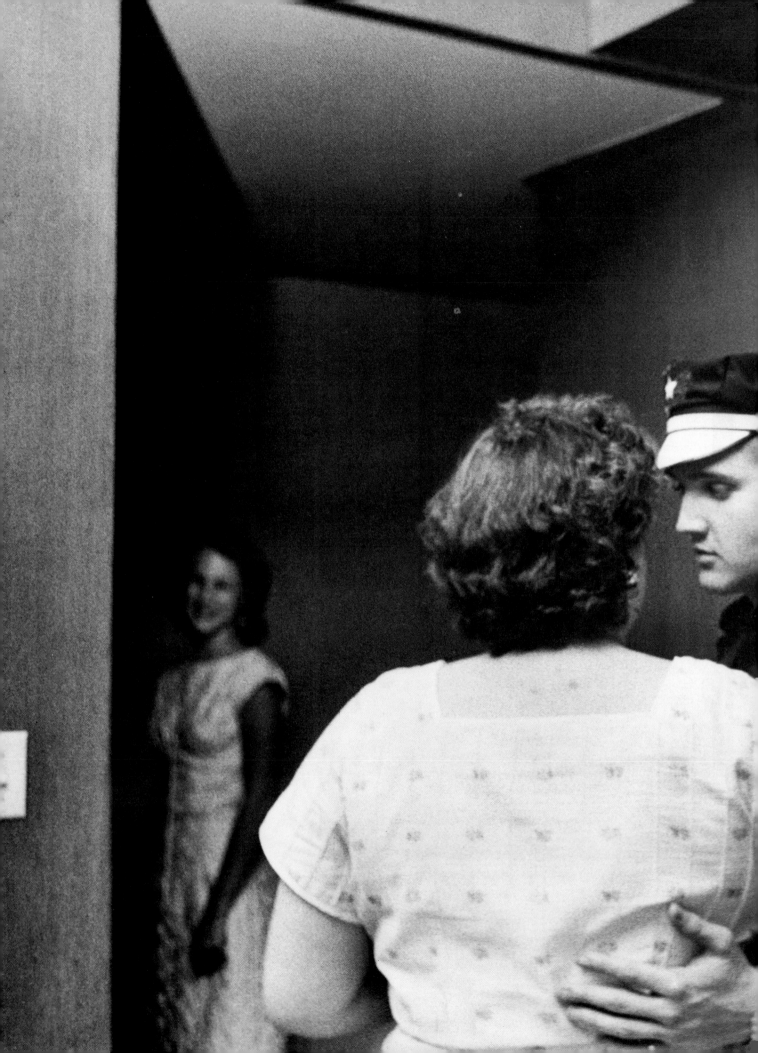

(Preceding page) Home. Elvis puts on his motorcycle cap and tells his mother not to worry. July 4, 1956.

Signing autographs in his backyard for some neighborhood fans.

(Following page) The girls continue to press him for autographs while a friend fiddles with the carburetor.

A supreme emblem of the fifties in America: a rock and roll rebel on a Harley-Davidson. He wonders why it won't start.

Elvis tries out the cycle in his backyard before maneuvering past his friends and neighbors watching from the carport.

Elvis' mother, Gladys, at left, watches over the family from the patio. Vernon and Elvis (below) after completing inspection of their new pool: the pump still doesn't work.

After a motorcycle ride interrupted by running out of gas, Elvis has a Pepsi on the back patio with his cousin, Bobby Smith, and his father, Vernon.

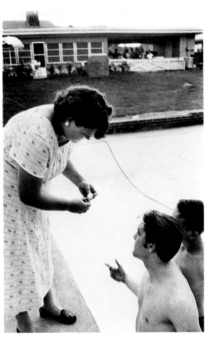

After diving into a
half-full pool, Elvis
waves off his
playmates and
calls for his moth-
er. He forgot
to take off his
watch. Mother as-
sures her son that
it's all right, she'll
take care of it.

135

After spending a day and a half on the train, Elvis lets it loose in his pool.

(Following page) A quiet moment with his father: this was the first chance Elvis had to relax in a week.

(Preceding page) Elvis poses for a cousin. The relatives had gathered at the Presley home for the Fourth of July and to attend his ben- efit concert at Russwood Sta- dium that night. Left to right: Elvis; Billy Smith, Elvis' cousin; Travis Smith, Gladys' brother and Billy's father; Vernon (shaving in back- ground); on the couch, Gladys and Minnie, Vernon's mother.

Before getting
ready for the
evening's concert,
Elvis shows his
mother a recent
photograph of
himself and thanks
her for a clean
pair of shorts.

In the family
living room,
grandmother Min-
nie, who lived
with Elvis, and
Barbara Hearn,
Elvis' high school
sweetheart, listen
to his new record,
"Don't Be Cruel."

After a shower,
half-dressed, his
hair uncombed,
Elvis embraces
Barbara to the
song "Anyway
You Want Me."

(Following page)
Listening to "Don't
Be Cruel." Top:
the portrait of
Elvis is an oil
painting of his first
major publicity
still.

(Left) Colonel Parker, the man in the shadows. Russwood Stadium, Memphis, July 4, 1956.

(Top) Being ushered to the front row, Russwood. Left to right: (rear) Barbara Hearn, Minnie Presley, Vernon Presley; (front) Colonel Parker's brother-in-law, Gladys Presley.

(Above) The Colonel promotes his "boy," selling glossies suitable for framing after the concert.

Sheriff's deputies and the Shore Patrol shield Elvis on his way to the Russwood stage.

His arrival at the concert was preceded by over two hours of variety acts. When he took center stage before 14,000 people, he told them "I'm gonna show you what the real Elvis is like tonight." He did.